Presents

Learn Guitar 3
The Method For A New Generation

Written & Method By:
John McCarthy

T0056536

Adapted By: Jimmy Rutkowski
Supervising Editor: Joe Palombo
Music Transcribing & Engraving: Jimmy Rutkowski
Production Manager: John McCarthy
Layout, Graphics & Design: Jimmy Rutkowski
Photography: Rodney Dabney
Copy Editors: Cathy McCarthy

Cover Art Direction & Design:
Jimmy Rutkowsk

HL14041756
ISBN: 978-1-4584-2473-0
Produced by The Rock House Method®

Table of Contents

Words From the Author

Music is a never ending journey. This is one of the great things I love about it. You can always find new ways to challenge your mind creatively and fingers physically. In this book you will be challenged with new scales and techniques and how to use these tools to improvise and write music. I've put together a well balanced program that will help you understand the theory of music and guide you through lead and rhythm examples. You will learn how to apply everything you have learned so far to develop your own unique style.

Grab your guitar and prepare to enter into the elite advanced level of guitar!

John McCarthy

Digital eBook

When you register this product at the lesson support site RockHouseSchool.com, you will receive a digital version of this book. This interactive eBook can be used on all devices that support Adobe PDF. This will allow you to access your book using the latest portable technology any time you want.

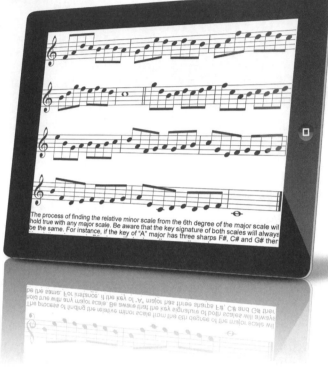

The Rock House Method Learning System

This learning system can be used on your own or guided by a teacher. Be sure to register for your free lesson support at RockHouseSchool.com. Your member number can be found inside the cover of this book.

Lesson Support **Site:** Once registered, you can use this fully interactive site along with your product to enhance your learning experience, expand your knowledge, link with instructors, and connect with a community of people around the world who are learning to play music using The Rock House Method®.

Gear Education Video: Walking into a music store can be an intimidating endeavor for someone starting out. To help you, Rock House has a series of videos to educate you on some of the gear you will encounter as you start your musical journey.

Quizzes: Each level of the curriculum contains multiple quizzes to gauge your progress. When you see a quiz icon go to the *Lesson Support* site and take the quiz. It will be graded and emailed to you for review.

Audio Examples & Play Along Tracks: Demonstrations of how each lesson should sound and full band backing tracks to play certain lessons over. These audio tracks are available on the accompanying CD as well as the *Lesson Support* site.

Icon Key

These tell you there is additional information and learning utilities available at RockHouseSchool.com to support that lesson.

Backing Track

CD Track Backing track icons are placed on lessons where there is an audio demonstration to let you hear what that lesson should sound like or a backing track to play the lesson over. Use these audio tracks to guide you through the lessons. **This is an mp3 CD, it can be played on any computer and all mp3 disc compatible playback devices.**

Metronome

Metronome icons are placed next to the examples that we recommend you practice using a metronome. You can download a free, adjustable metronome on the *Lesson Support* site.

Worksheet

Worksheets are a great tool to help you thoroughly learn and understand music. These worksheets can be downloaded at the *Lesson Support* site.

Tuner

You can download the free online tuner on the *Lesson Support* site to help tune your instrument.

Three Notes Per String

SCALE PROFESSOR

Now it's time to learn the natural minor scales in a new perspective. I'm going to show you seven positions each starting from a different note of the scale. These are three notes per string scale patterns in the key of "A." There are some five fret stretches that will require special fingerings to make the scale easier to play. Follow the fingering below each tablature staff.

1st Position

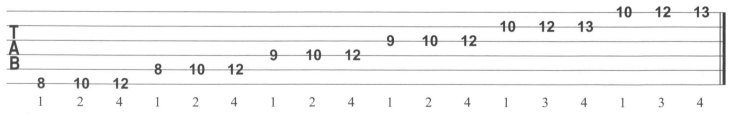

2nd Position

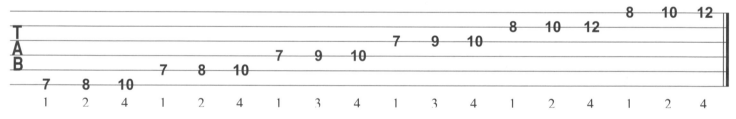

3rd Position

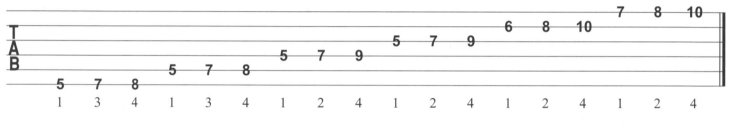

6

4th Position

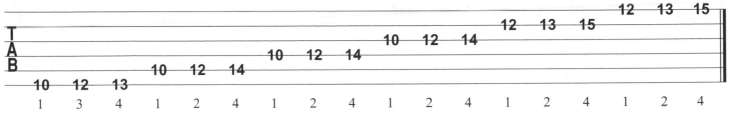

1   3   4   1   2   4   1   2   4   1   2   4   1   2   4   1   2   4

5th Position

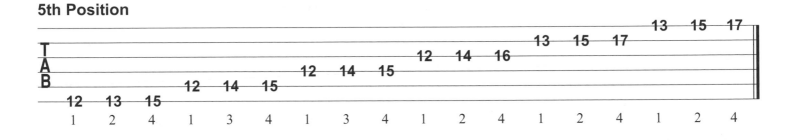

1   2   4   1   3   4   1   3   4   1   2   4   1   2   4   1   2   4

6th Position

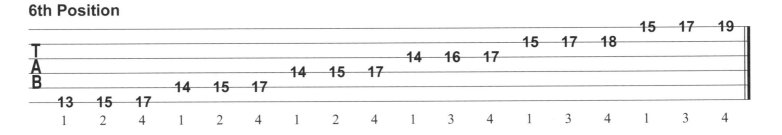

1   2   4   1   2   4   1   2   4   1   3   4   1   3   4   1   3   4

7th Position

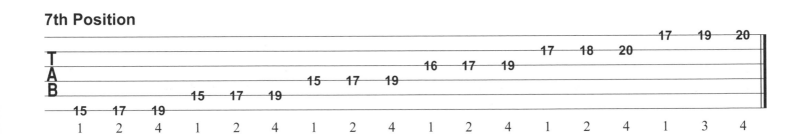

1   2   4   1   2   4   1   2   4   1   2   4   1   2   4   1   3   4

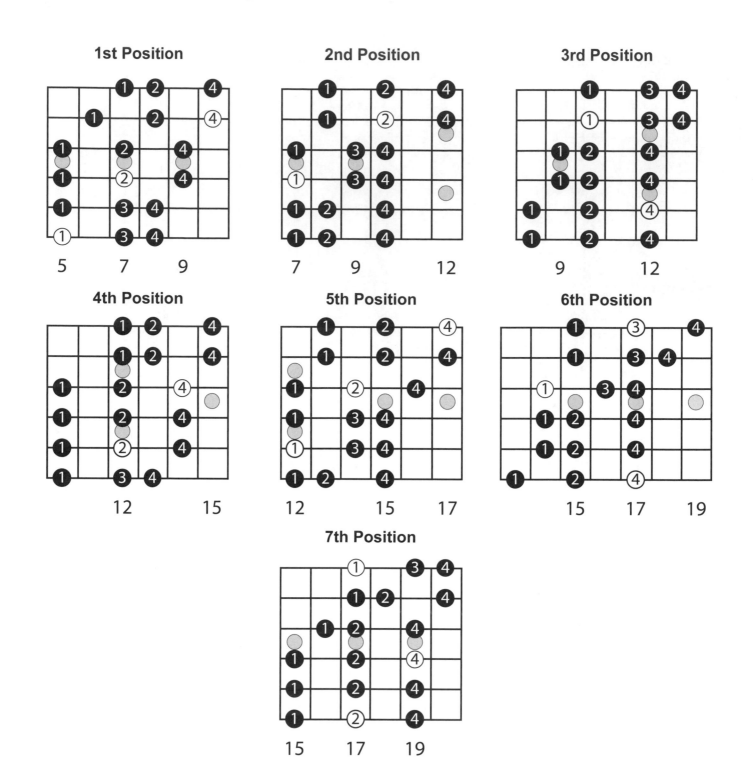

1st Position

5   7   9

2nd Position

7   9   12

3rd Position

9   12

4th Position

12   15

5th Position

12   15   17

6th Position

15   17   19

7th Position

15   17   19

Learning scales in different perspectives will help you master them. Three notes per string scales are easy to apply in sequential patterns across the neck.

 **MUSIC ASSIGNMENT**

Once you have these scales memorized in the key of "A" start transposing them into other keys. I recommend next learning the key of "E" because it is a very popular key for guitar players. The first position in E will start on the open 6th string or 12th fret an octave higher.

The Gallop Rhythm

The gallop rhythm is used in many genres of music. To break it down rhythmically it would be an eighth note followed by two sixteenths.

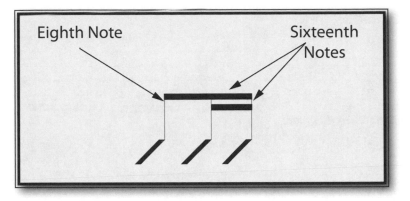

This rhythm creates a bouncy feel that is reminiscent of a horse galloping; hence the name, "Gallop Rhythm." The way you would count this rhythm comes from the sixteenth note counting. First count sixteenth notes: 1 – e – & – ah then take out the e from the count to form the gallop count:

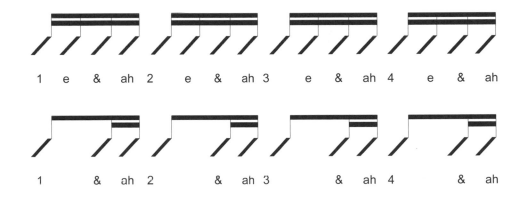

Now apply this rhythm to the entire progression below:

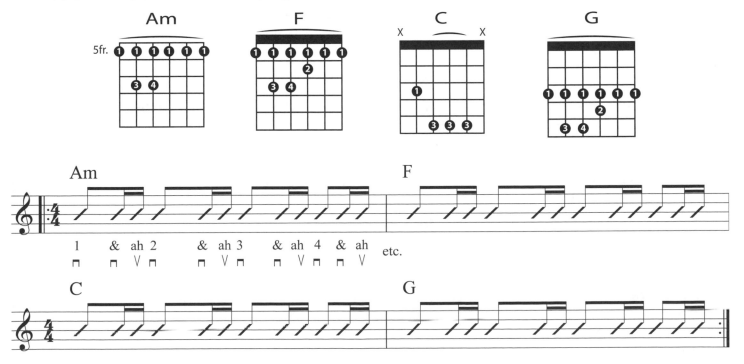

Natural Minor Lead Patterns

CD Track 4-5

Lead patterns are a great way to get familiar with a scale. The following lead patterns are from the A natural minor three note per string scale and played using sixteenth note and triplet patterns:

1st Position Sixteenth Lead Pattern

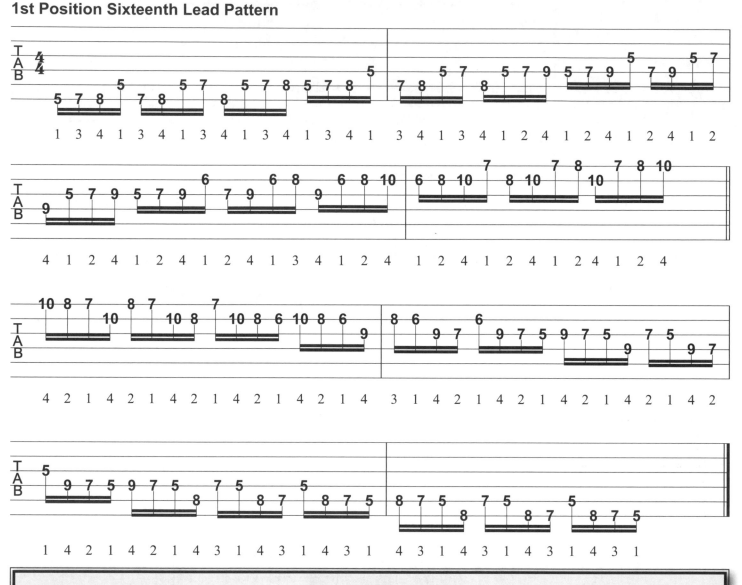

Pick Variations

You must consistently challenge your picking technique. A great exercise to use as you play these lead patterns is to practice them with three different pick variations.

1. All down picking – First play the lead patterns using all down picking. It is important to have a strong down pick. Many times when you want to accent a section within a melody or lead you would use a series of down picks.

2. Alternate picking – To play fast passages seemlessly you need to have alternate picking down cold. This should be second nature.

3. All up picking – Many players never practice picking all up. It is important to have your up pick as dominant as your down pick to have an even alternate pick technique. It may feel awkward at first but stick with it and it will pay off.

1st Position Triplet Lead Pattern

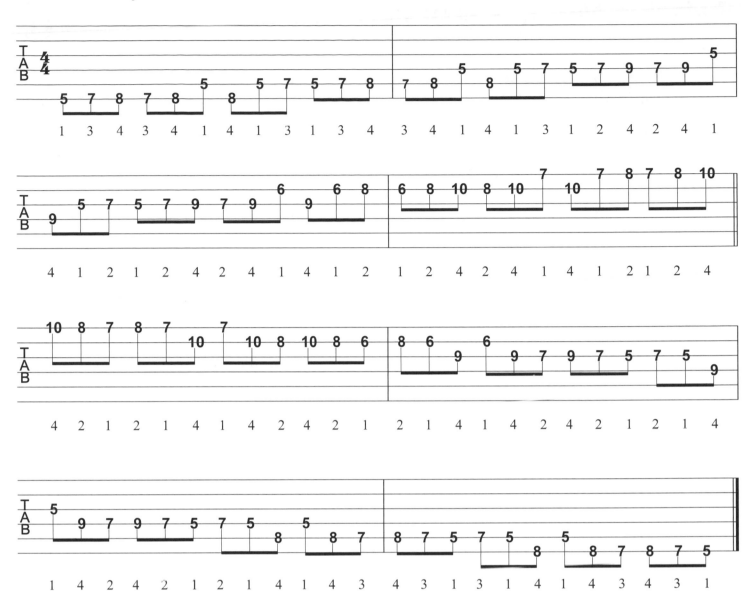

MUSIC ASSIGNMENT

After you feel comfortable playing these patterns transpose them to all seven scale positions in the key of "A." Watch the fingering because there will be some tricky sections. Next apply these lead patterns over the "Gallop Rhythm." It's important to use these in a creative manner.

Relative Minor Theory

Every major scale has a relative minor scale that is built starting from the 6th degree. They are called "relative minor" scales because they share the same exact notes. The only difference is the order of the notes. This is a big difference because this changes the tone center and root note which will make it sound like a completely different scale. Below is a C major scale and its relative minor scale, A minor. As you see, all the notes are completely the same. Just the order is different. Play through these two scales now and pay attention to how the same notes in a different order sound different.

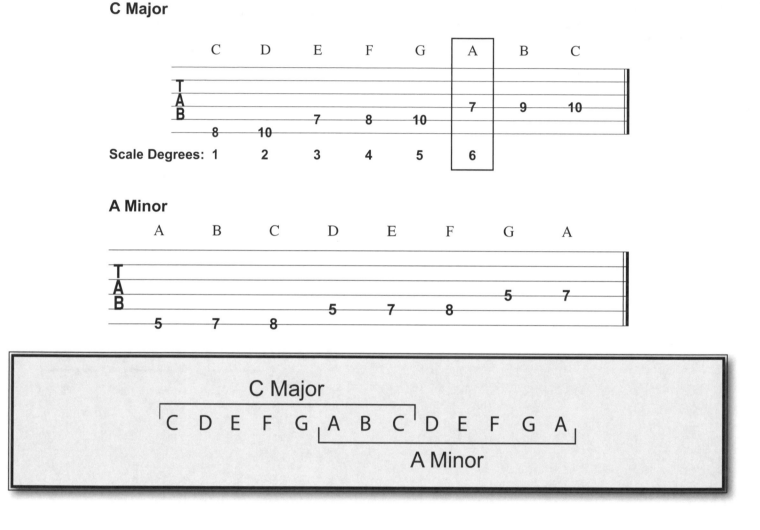

C Major

Scale Degrees: 1 2 3 4 5 6

A Minor

The process of finding the relative minor scale from the 6th degree of the major scale will hold true with any major scale. Be aware that the key signature of both scales will always be the same. For instance, if the key of "A" major has three sharps F♯, C♯ and G♯ then it's relative minor scale F♯ minor will also have the same three sharps.

MUSIC ASSIGNMENT

Your assignment is to write a chart of all the sharped major scales and their relative minor. Memorize which scales are related because they will be used together often when writing songs and melodies. On the next page I have outlined all the scales with their relative minor so you can check your work. Use the blank relative minor chart available from the *Lesson Support* site for this assignment.

Relative Minor Scales – Sharped Keys

Below are the sharped major keys with their respective relative minor scales. Notice how the two scales have the same notes. The relative minor scale is just expanding the major scale using the same notes in a different order.

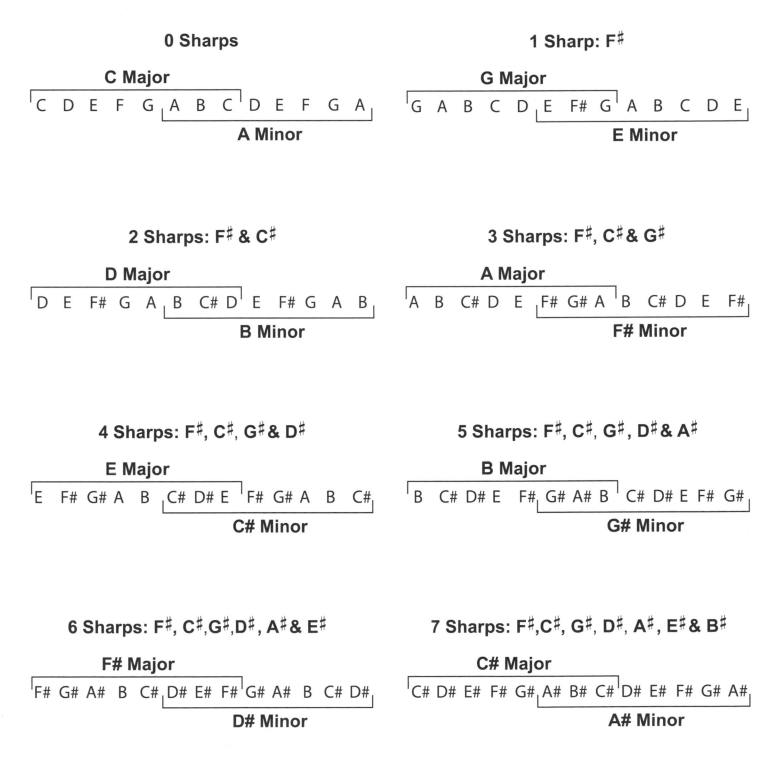

0 Sharps

C Major

C D E F G A B C D E F G A

A Minor

1 Sharp: F♯

G Major

G A B C D E F# G A B C D E

E Minor

2 Sharps: F♯ & C♯

D Major

D E F# G A B C# D E F# G A B

B Minor

3 Sharps: F♯, C♯ & G♯

A Major

A B C# D E F# G# A B C# D E F#

F# Minor

4 Sharps: F♯, C♯, G♯ & D♯

E Major

E F# G# A B C# D# E F# G# A B C#

C# Minor

5 Sharps: F♯, C♯, G♯, D♯ & A♯

B Major

B C# D# E F# G# A# B C# D# E F# G#

G# Minor

6 Sharps: F♯, C♯, G♯, D♯, A♯ & E♯

F# Major

F# G# A# B C# D# E# F# G# A# B C# D#

D# Minor

7 Sharps: F♯, C♯, G♯, D♯, A♯, E♯ & B♯

C# Major

C# D# E# F# G# A# B# C# D# E# F# G# A#

A# Minor

Creating Melodies

Time to get creative! For this lesson I've provided an A minor progression that you will create melodies over using the natural minor scales in the key of "A." Start by playing the progression to get familiar with its sound then improvise over the full band backing track rhythm. Improvising is not easy and it will take practice to be able to create melodies. Start by just playing the scales over the progression forwards and back, then mix up the notes and find your own interesting note combinations.

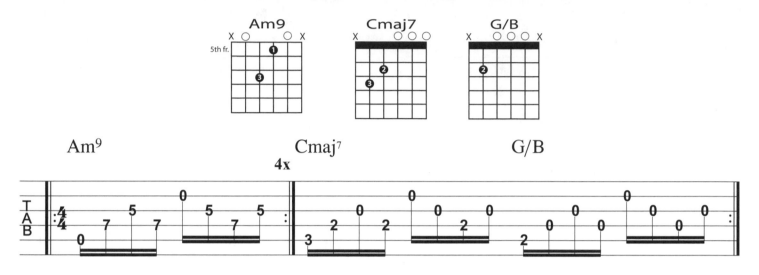

Here is an example to get you started. This example comes from the natural minor scale first position. Use this as a starting point and expand upon this idea and start creating your own melodies.

Example 1

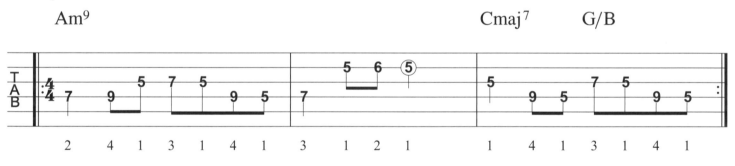

Example 2

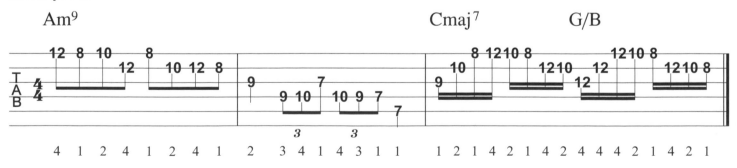

Finger Picking Progression

House of the Rising Sun

Here is a common finger picking pattern that can be used in many progressions. There are variations for the pattern, each different to follow the bass note of the chord. Practice the basic patterns on open strings before you apply it to the chords.

Pattern 1

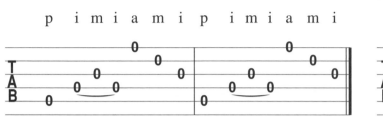

Pattern 2

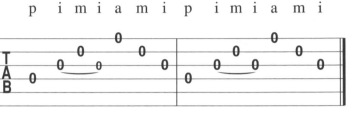

bpm: **70**

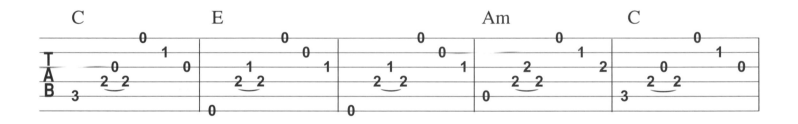

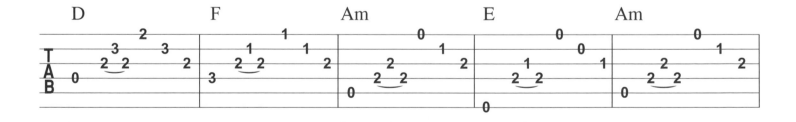

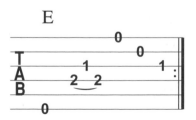

15

Natural Minor Scale Full Neck View

It's important to know your scales in different keys. By practicing them in all keys you will get the knowledge needed to play them in any song or lead. You should learn these scales as individual patterns then begin to see the entire neck as a whole. Below are the natural minor scales in the key of "A" in a full neck diagram. See how all the patterns you learned earlier are found within this diagram.

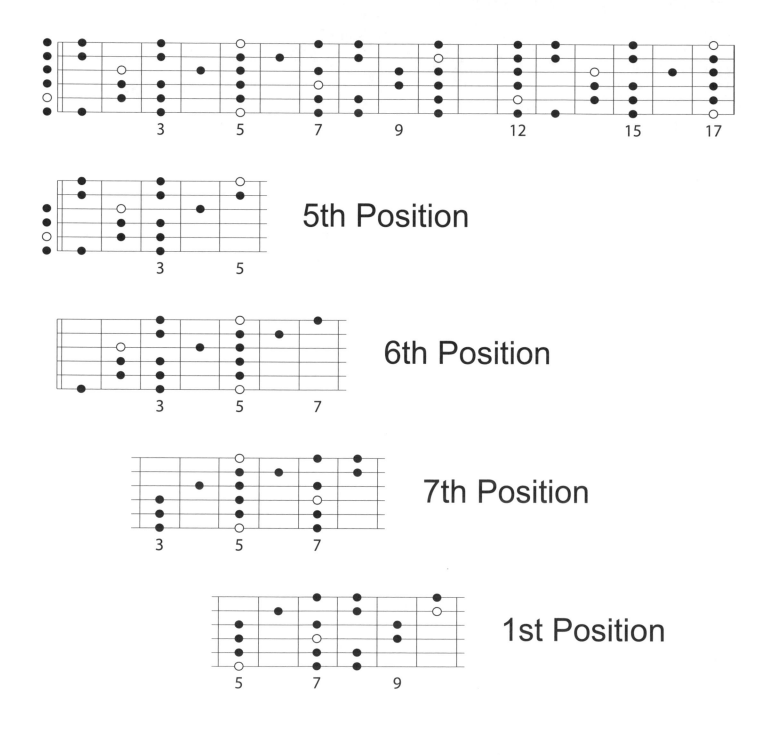

5th Position

6th Position

7th Position

1st Position

16

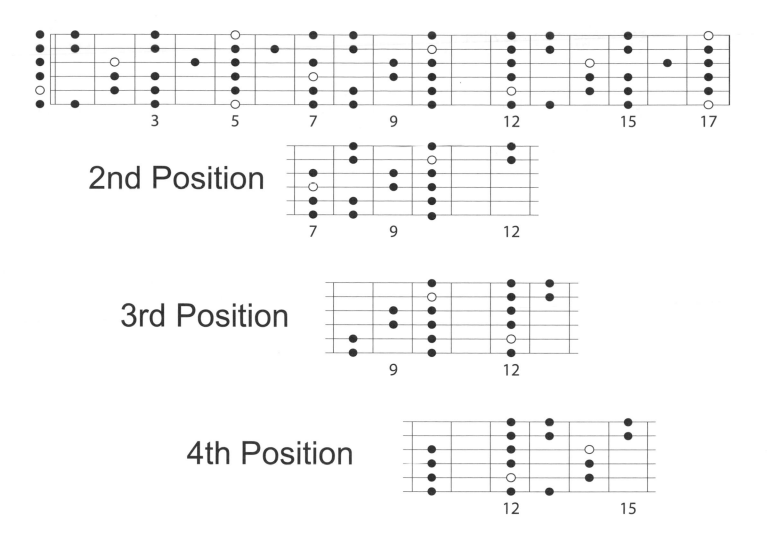

2nd Position

3rd Position

4th Position

Next, you will learn the three note per string scale patterns in the key of "E." Below is the full neck diagram for the E natural minor scales, write out where each position falls within this full neck diagram to help memorize them in this key:

Key of "E"

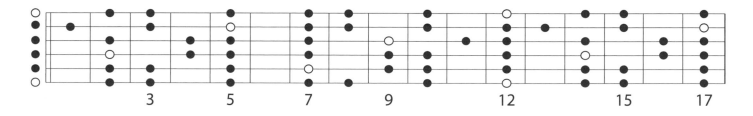

MUSIC ASSIGNMENT

Your next step to scale mastery is to write these scales out in all seven keys A – B – C – D – E – F – G in both scale patterns and full neck diagram as they were in this lesson. You can download blank scale pattern and full neck diagrams to use for this assignment. Next, start a daily regimen of practicing these scales in a different key each day. Here is a good daily schedule to follow:

Monday A, Tuesday C, Wednesday E, Thursday G, Friday B
Saturday D, Sunday F

Blues Slide Rhythm

This blues rhythm in the key of "C" minor has slides that accent the $\flat 7$ note for each chord. The $\flat 7$ note makes each chord have a dominant 7th sound which is used often in blues music. This rhythm follows a classic 1 – 4 – 5 progression which helps to make this a great blues progression. Be sure to play this with the bass and drum backing track and have some fun!

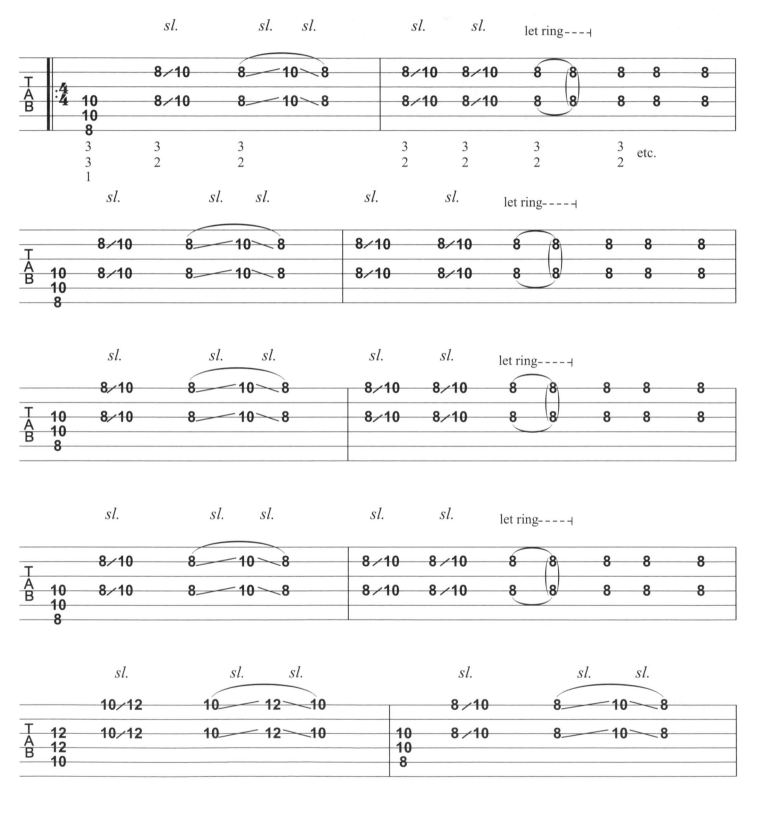

18

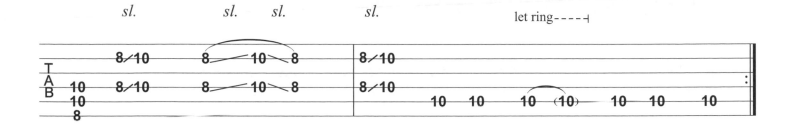

MUSIC ASSIGNMENT

Below are all 5 positions of the minor pentatonic scales in the key of "C" across the neck. Play all these scales over this progression and create some cool blues leads.

Key of C Minor Pentatonic Scales

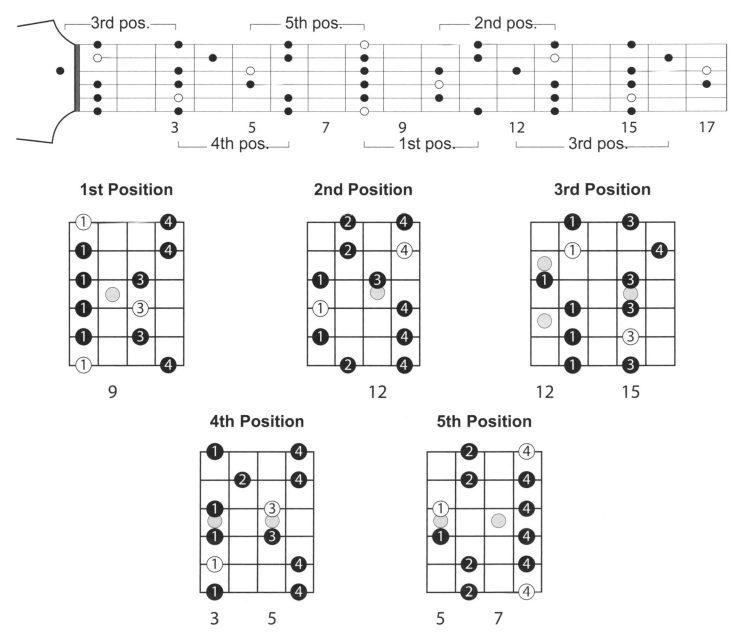

Exercise Workout Routine

Here is a full exercise routine to strengthen your fingers and make them more coordinated. Practice each with a metronome and make sure to play clean at all times before speeding up. A daily exercise routine will ensure fast, effective learning.

Ultimate Speed

This is an alternate picking exercise that will help you learn to move laterally up the neck. Pick every note using alternate picking and continue to move the same pattern up to the 12th fret and back down to the 5th fret.

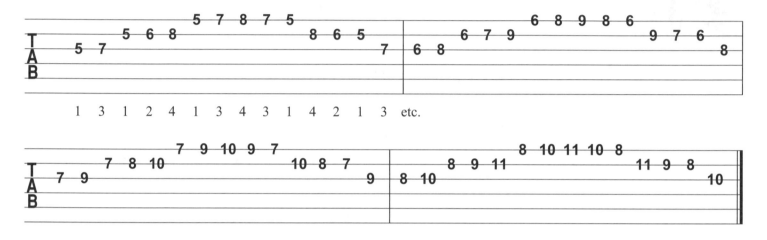

Open String Speed Pick

The trick to this exercise is to keep your picking moving with consistent alternate picking. The open strings allow you to gain speed easily. The second line moves down the neck using the 3rd string open between each note.

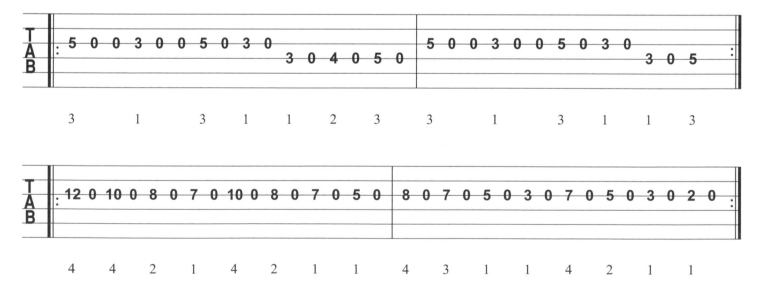

Finger Crusher #2

This is a two string lateral exercise. It is also a great endurance exercise. The first measure of each two string pattern comes from the second position minor pentatonic scale. Use a metronome and play through from each two string sequence in a row without stopping.

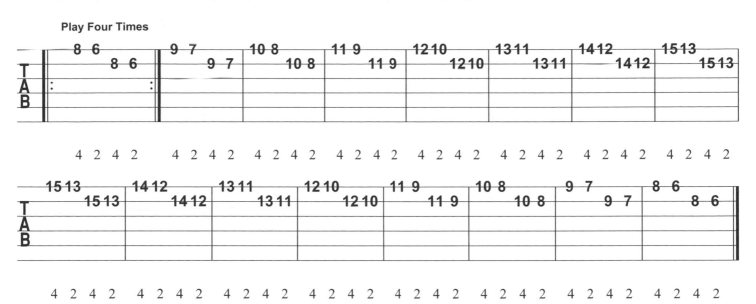

Below are the four remaining two string groupings from the 2nd position minor pentatonic scale. Use the pattern above to play through each of these groupings:

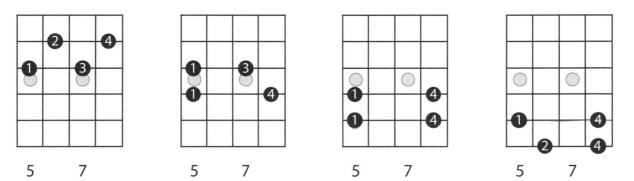

3rd & 4th Finger Stinger

This exercise isolates the 3rd and 4th fingers which are the two fingers hardest to coordinate. Make sure to pick each finger up before picking the next, never having two fingers down at a time. Use alternate picking and build speed gradually.

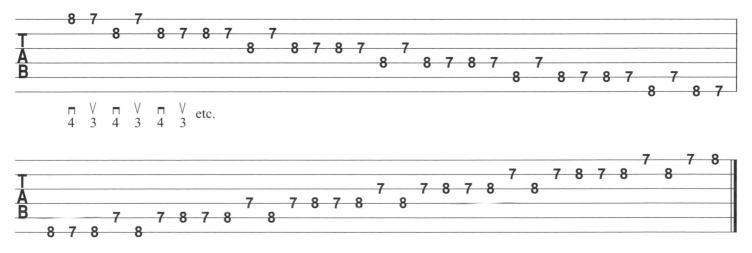

Practice Tips

To ensure constant progress and high motivation you have to develop practice habits that will keep you interested and challenged. Great practice habits will result in better overall playing and take you to the next level. As you move forward with your practice routine there are a few things you should do:

1. Practice Consistently
I have had many students come to me and say I missed four days of practice and on the fifth day I played 4 hours. This is not the way to practice and see results because you do not give your fingers a chance to gain muscle memory. Practice every day even if it is for a short amount of time, be consistent.

2. Practice Area
Have a practice spot set up so you can have privacy to focus on your playing. It is a great idea to have a music stand to help position your music so you can sit comfortably. I remember when I started playing and I would lay my music on my bed and twist my neck to try to read and hold my guitar up properly, it was a real pain in the neck!

3. Keep your Guitar in Sight
Always have your guitar out of the case, I use the expression "out of sight out of mind." If you see your guitar sitting there on a stand you are more prone to pick it up and play. When it's in a case under your bed its work to take it out and this may deter you from practicing. Besides when your friends come over your house and see your guitar they will be impressed!

4. Practice Schedule
Set a scheduled practice time each day. Say you want to practice before school or work everyday, make this time a routine then later in the day you can play for fun and jam a little more.

Creating a Practice Routine

As you evolve as a guitarist you will be constantly changing your practice outline. You should combine a series of components in your practice routine that will help you develop all aspects of your playing. Here is a list of my favorite types of exercises:

1. Technique Exercises for the Fretting Hand
This is an exercise that challenges the coordination of your fretting hand. Many hammer on and pull off exercises work well to develop your fretting hand. These are usually repetitive exercises like Finger Crusher #2. Build speed gradually and practice them with a metronome.

2. Technique Exercises for the Picking Hand
This is an exercise that challenges the coordination of your pick hand. Multiple string repetitive sequences are great pick exercises. You should build speed gradually and practice these with a metronome.

3. Scales and Patterns
Use seven note and pentatonic scales in all different keys. Practice them with patterns of 2's, 3's and 4's always using alternate picking. Mix it up week by week to challenge your fingers.

4. Performance Pieces

This would be a song that you wish to learn that you haven't started yet. Pick a song that you want to learn and have it on CD or tab and start picking it apart…literally!

5. Creating Leads Over Progressions (Backing Tracks)

This is where you get creative and jam a little to make melodies and leads. You can use jam backing tracks that have progressions of bass, drums and rhythm. Another way to do this is to pick your favorite CD and jam along pretending that you are a member of the band. Mimic the lead singer's melodies and play riffs and phrasings along with the track. This is a great way to learn to play melodically.

6. Classical Pieces

I like to use single string classical pieces like Mozart Sonata #11 or #16, they are almost always very challenging and they sound cool with a bit of distortion kicked in too.

7. Fun Playing

This is where you play things you know already, crank the amp up and rip into some guitar and have some fun!

8. Mental Perception (Visualization Away From Your Instrument)

Even though you may not be able to have your guitar with you all day long, every day, that doesn't mean you can't practice. Visualization is so important. Just going through your scales and the notes on the neck in your mind paints a visual picture that will help you to fly across the strings with ease. When you can see it in your mind your fingers will follow.

Canon Progression

CD Track
12-13

Here is a "Canon Progression" with an arpeggiated picking pattern. Practice the picking pattern for each chord slowly first, then put it all together with the bass and drum backing track.

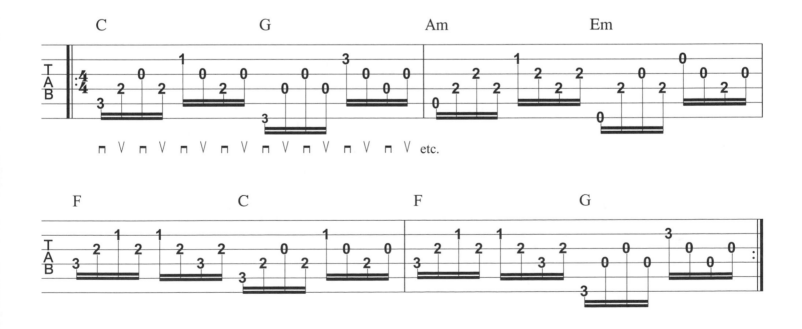

23

Canon Octave Melody

We are going to use the rhythm from the "Canon Progression" lesson and create an octave melody. Below is the basic melody I created, play this first and get familiar with its sound:

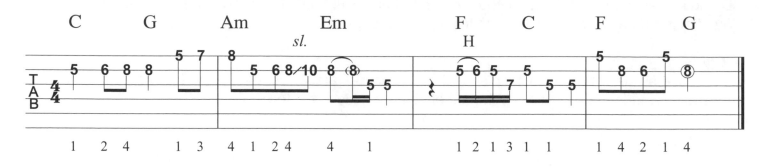

Below is the octave melody variation. Make sure to deaden the middle string in each octave shape and strum all three strings. Notice how the octave melody stands out.

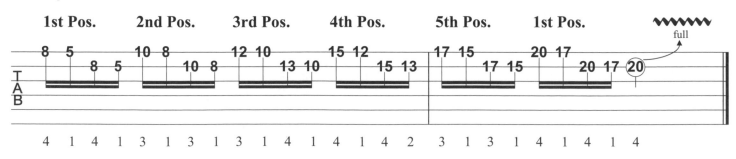

Two String Lateral Runs

Pentatonic scales have a unique sound and because there are less notes then the full minor scale it is important to find creative ways to play these scales across the neck. These two string lateral runs let you see how you can apply a lateral approach to the scales. For this example they will be in the key of "A" minor. The following are the first two examples:

Example 1

Example 2

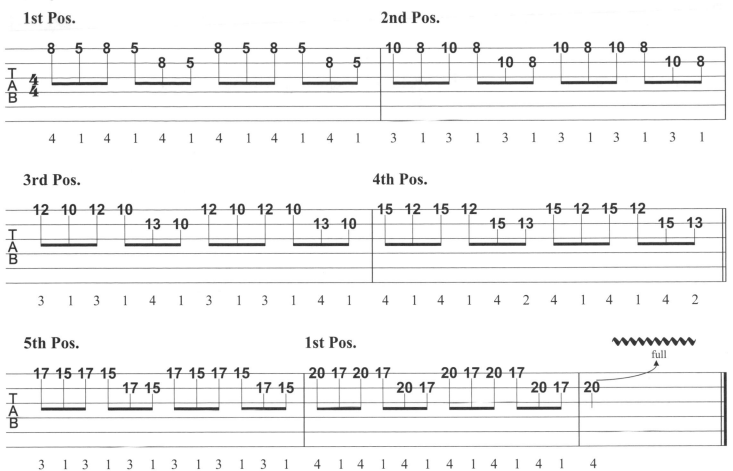

1st Pos.   **2nd Pos.**

3rd Pos.   **4th Pos.**

5th Pos.   **1st Pos.**

MUSIC ASSIGNMENT

Now that you feel comfortable with these patterns transpose them to the other strings 2 & 3, 3 & 4, 4 & 5, 5 & 6. Make sure to write these out in tablature to reinforce the patterns in your memory.

Once you have them played smoothly across the neck apply them over the "House of the Rising Sun" rhythm or any other A minor rhythm you learned from previous lessons. Below is example 1 applied to the 2nd and 3rd strings:

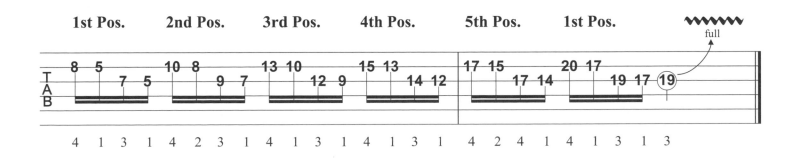

Riff Challenge #1

CD Track
17-21

Here are a few riffs to challenge your fingers. Remember that these riffs are created from the scales so be aware of the key and scale position.

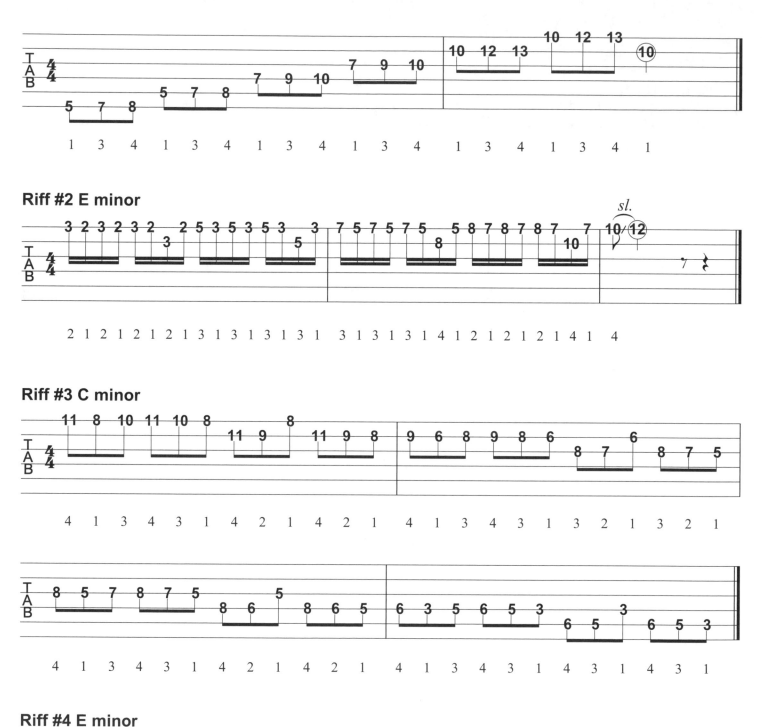

Riff #2 E minor

Riff #3 C minor

Riff #4 E minor

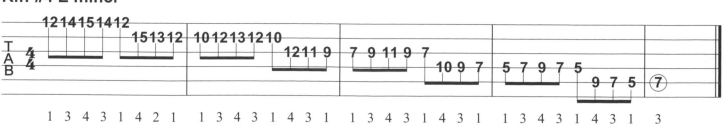

Riff #5 A minor

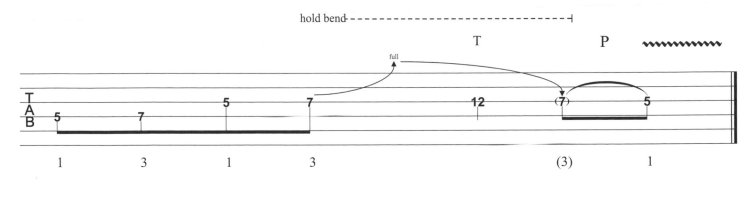

Lead Techniques – Bending

A player's bending technique has a very unique sound. This helps them create their own signature as a player. In this lesson you will learn some advanced bending techniques. These will be great to use in creating your own leads or learning one of your favorites.

Half Step Bend

Half step bends are especially useful for soloing with blues scales. Train your ear to hear the difference between whole step and half step bends; eventually your fingers will instinctively know how much to bend the strings to achieve the correct pitches.

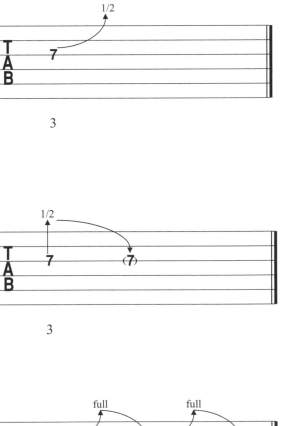

Ghost Bend

Ghost bends (sometimes referred to as pre-bends) are performed by bending the note to the proper pitch before striking the note. In this example, pre-bend the note a half step and then pick the note and gradually release the note to its original pitch.

Double Pump Bend

You also bend and release the same note repeatedly without picking it again. The following example uses a bend-release-bend-release pattern. This technique can be used in a variety of ways.

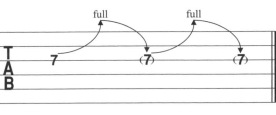

Scream Bend

To perform the following scream bend, pick both notes simultaneously and bend just the lower note up a whole step. Keep the higher note stationary and allow it to ring out along with the bend.

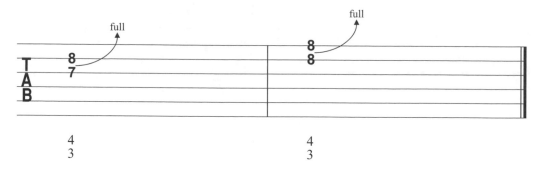

MUSIC ASSIGNMENT

The examples in this lesson were in the key of "A," transpose these to the key of "E." Apply them into your playing. You must use new techniques as much as possible to make them come natural when you are creating your own leads or melodies. In the next lesson you will use these bend techniques in a complete lead.

CD Track

26-28

Complete Lead in E Minor

In this lesson you will be applying the tapping and bending techniques you learned in a complete lead. Practice this lead in small sections repetitively then put it all together. Be sure to use the full band backing track to play the lead over. Learn the rhythm below before you take on the lead:

Rhythm:

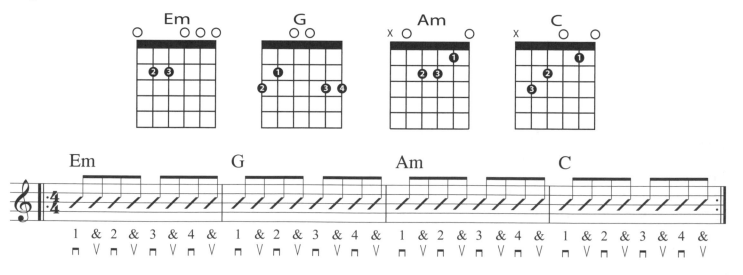

Lead: Key of "Em"

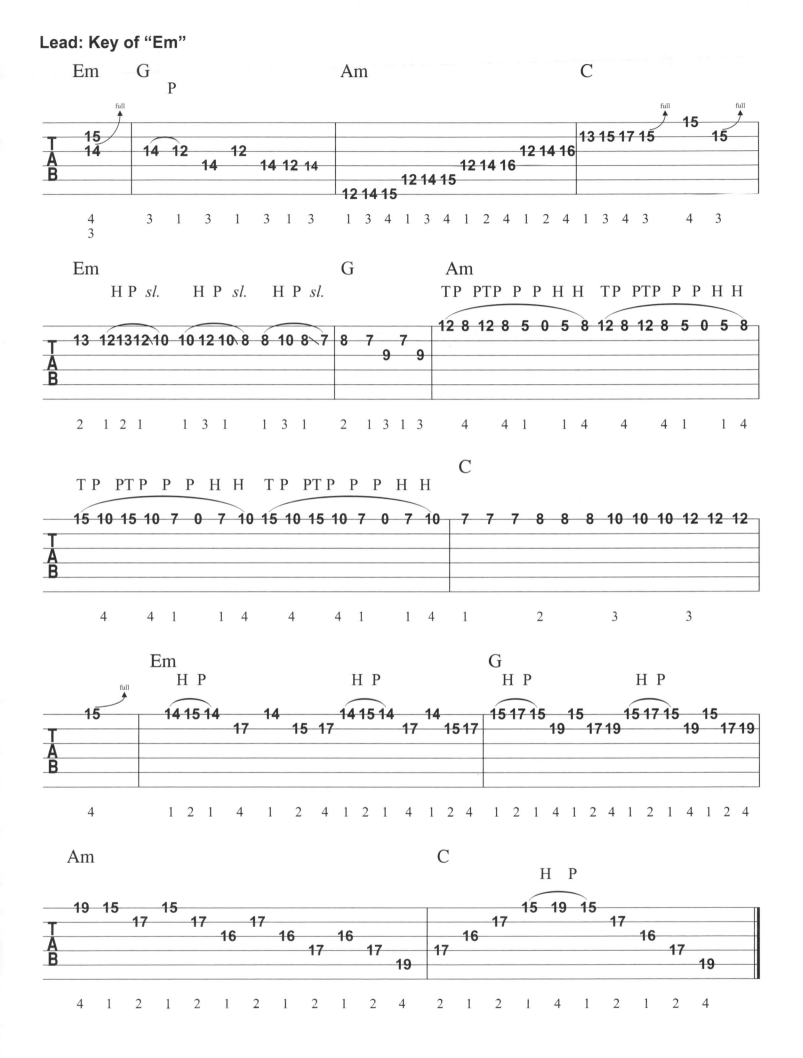

Multi Position Lead Patterns

CD Track
29-31

It's important to visualize the entire neck while you are playing a lead. Learning the scales laterally gives you another perspective in addition to the block patterns you have learned. In this lesson you will learn how to move laterally across three scale positions of the A minor pentatonic scales in a triplet and eighth note pattern. After you can play these easily forwards and backwards play them over the full band backing track.

Positions 1-3 Eighth Notes

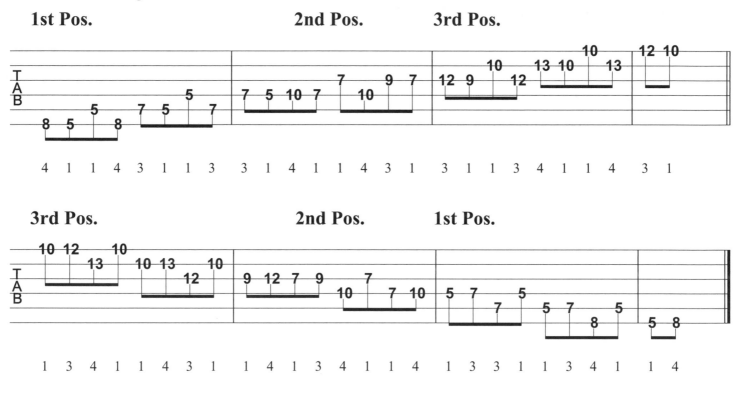

Positions 1-3 Triplets

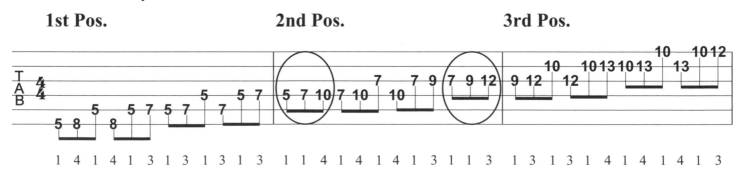

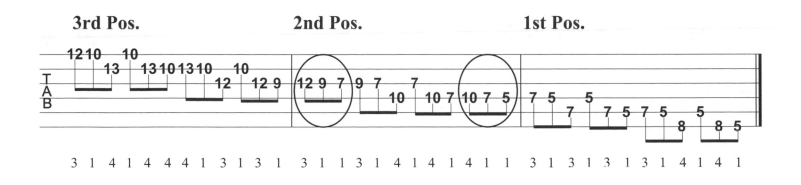

Positions 1-3 Sixteenth Notes

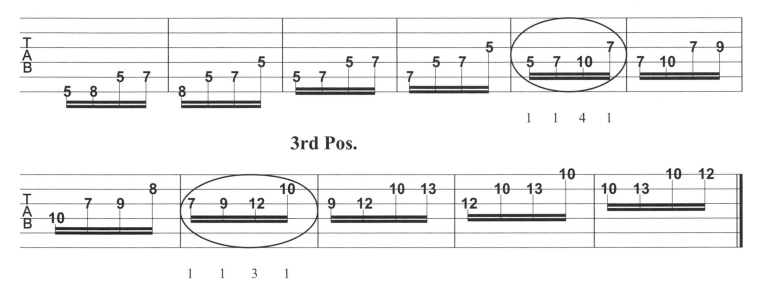

MUSIC ASSIGNMENT

Once you have these patterns memorized transpose them to the key of "E" and play them over a backing track. You can use the full band backing track from the previous lesson or any other progression in the key of "E" minor. Add some bends and melodic phrasings within these lead patterns and you'll see how easy it can be to create a great lead.

Learn Guitar 3 - Quiz 1

Once you complete this section go to RockHouseSchool.com and take the quiz to track your progress. You will receive an email with your results and suggestions.

Chord Construction

Major 7th & Minor 7th Chords

CHORD PROFESSOR

Major and minor 7th chords are used in many genres of music. They, however, don't sound as pleasant with heavy distortion. They seem to come alive with a clean sound or light distortion. Major 7th chords contain the 1st – 3rd and 5th of the major scale like the major chord but with the 7th degree added. Here is how these chords are created from a C major scale:

C Major Scale: C - D - E - F - G - A - B - C

                     1   2   3   4   5   6   7   8

C Major 7th (CM7): C - E - G - B

Major 7th Chord Formula: 1   3   5   7

To form a minor 7th chord take the same four notes of the major 7th chord but flat the 3rd and 7th degrees. The notes of a Cm7th chord are C – E♭ – G – B♭.

C minor 7th (Cm7): C - E♭ - G - B♭

Minor 7th Chord Formula: 1   ♭3   5   ♭7

The following are CM7th and Cm7th chords with the scale degrees listed at the bottom. Notice the two notes that are different are the ♭3 and ♭7 notes.

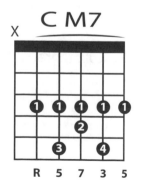

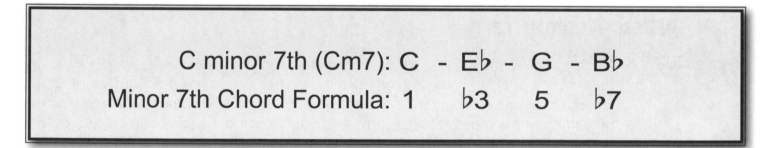

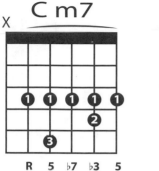
C m7

R 5 ♭7 ♭3 5

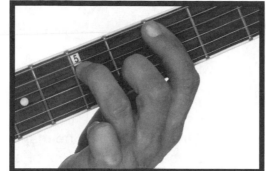

MUSIC ASSIGNMENT

You also need to get your ears familiar with the sound of a Major 7th and minor 7th chord. Strum each chord and let it ring out. Really listen to the chord's characteristics. They each have a unique sound that you must know and be able to decipher. You can also use the *Chord Ear Trainer* on the *Lesson Support* site to test your ear development.

Major 7th Chord Progression

CD Track

32-33

This chord progression uses two major 7th chords you learned in Book 2. The rhythm for this progression is syncopated and incorporates a ghost strum. Make sure to play this progression over the bass and drum backing track.

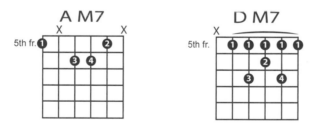

A M7   D M7

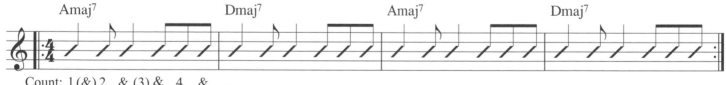

Count: 1 (&) 2 & (3) & 4 & etc.
Strum: ⊓   ⊓   V V ⊓ V

MUSIC ASSIGNMENT

Once you have played this progression over the bass and drum backing track experiment with variations with the strum pattern. Create your own patterns. Make sure to keep your strum arm loose and relaxed.

Major Scales Key of "C"

SCALE PROFESSOR

In this lesson we will go through all five positions of the major scale that span the entire neck in the key of "C." The notes that make the C major scale are C – D – E – F – G – A – B. These five scale positions consist of these 7 notes played across the neck. After you go through each position play the root notes within each. These are going to be the most important notes because they are the tone center.

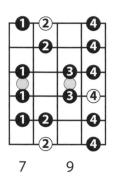

1st Position

```
                                    7 810  10 8 7
T                            810            10 8
A                      7 910                 10 9 7
B               7 910                              10 9 7
         7 810                                      10 8 7
    810                                                  10 8

    2 4 1 2 4 1 3 4 1 3 4 2 4 1 2 4    4 2 1 4 2 4 3 1 4 3 1 4 2 1 4 2
```

7   9

2nd Position

```
                                    101213  131210
T                            101213          131210
A                      9 1012                 12109
B               9 1012                         12109
         1012                                       1210
    101213                                            131210

    1 3 4 1 3 1 2 4 1 2 4 1 3 41  3 4    4 3 1 4 3 1 4 2 1 4 2 1 3 1 4 3 1
```

9   12

3rd Position

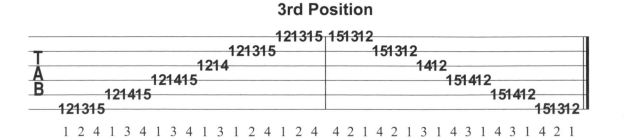

```
    1 2 4 1 3 4 1 3 4 1 3 1 2 4 1 2 4    4 2 1 4 2 1 3 1 4 3 1 4 3 1 4 2 1
```

12   15

34

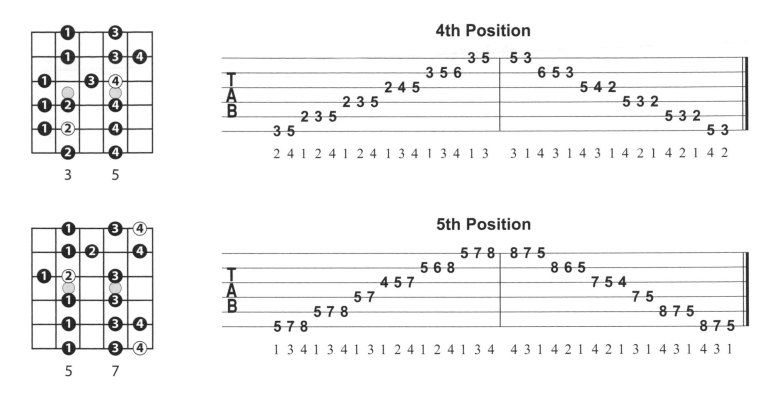

4th Position

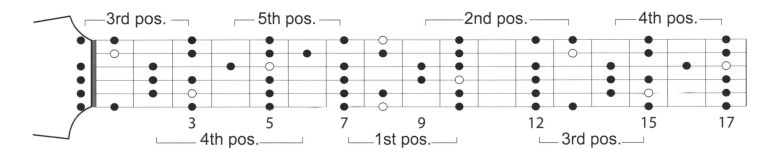

5th Position

Now let's look at the C major scales across the entire neck. Below is a full neck diagram. You can see each of the five positions you learned within this diagram. Make sure to see how they connect, the second half of one is the beginning of the next. It's important to start viewing the scales on the neck as a whole as well as in the positions you learned.

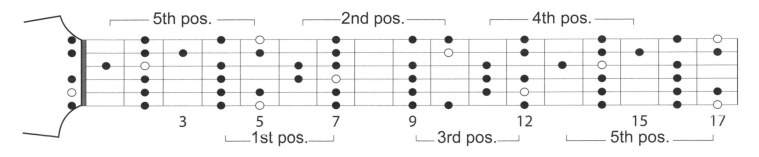

MUSIC ASSIGNMENT

Transpose these scales to the key of "A." The same exact position patterns will be used, just play them at different frets lining up all the root notes to A. The first scale position will start at the 5th fret. Below is the full neck diagram for the key of "A."

35

Minor 7th Chord Progression

This progression is a great example of minor blues. The two minor 7th chord fingerings you learned are used here, Bm7 is the I chord and Em7 the IV chord. The progression finishes with G7 and F#7 bar chords. Dominant seventh chords are commonly used in blues progressions.

The strum pattern has one dead or muted strum. Practice the strum pattern below with open strings before applying it to the chords. An "x" represents each dead strum.

Down – X – up down up down up.

Now apply this pattern to the complete progression. Make sure to play this over the bass and drum backing track.

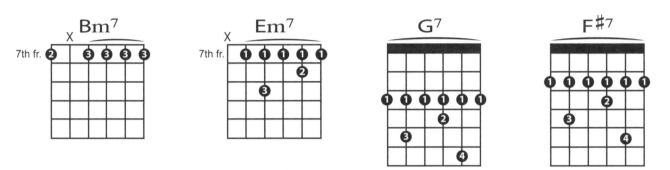

MUSIC ASSIGNMENT

This is a great progression to use the natural minor and minor pentatonic scales in the key of "B" to solo over. Both scales first position will start at the 7th fret. Play these scales over the full band backing track.

Lateral Runs Natural Minor

In this lesson you will play the natural minor scales in the key of "A" up each string. Playing patterns laterally will help you memorize the notes of these scales and see them in a new perspective. The two patterns in this lesson will be triplet and sixteenth note.

Example 1

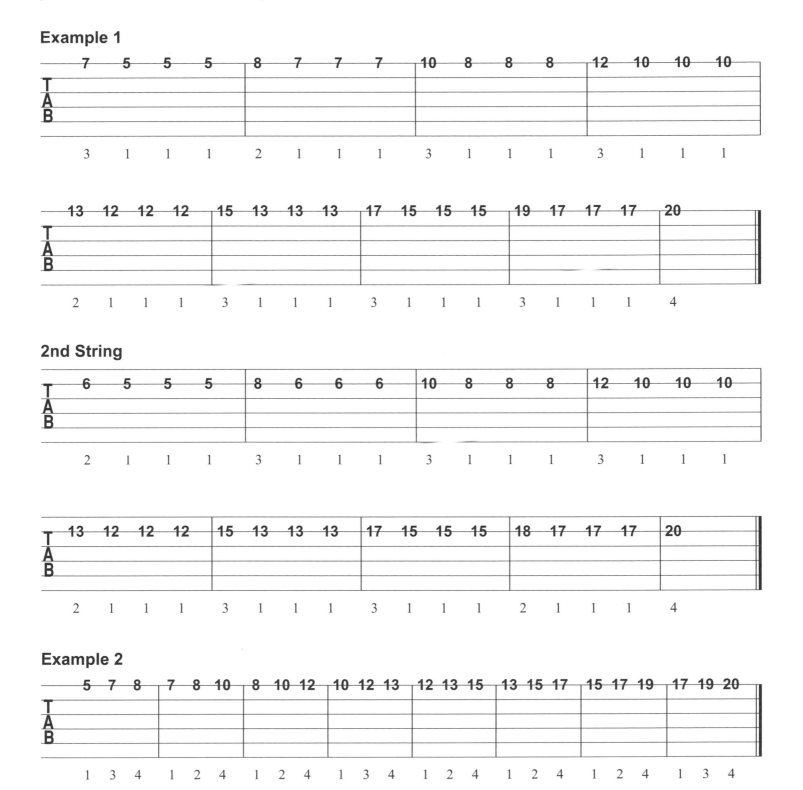

2nd String

Example 2

2nd String

T	5 6 8	6 8 10	8 10 12	10 12 13	12 13 15	13 15 17	15 17 18	17 18 20
A								
B								

1 2 4   1 2 4   1 2 4   1 3 4   1 2 4   1 2 4   1 3 4   1 2 4

MUSIC ASSIGNMENT

Once you have these two patterns memorized on the first two strings forwards and backwards use the same pattern on the last four strings. It's important to learn the scales on each string across the neck. After you can play them all in the key of "A" transpose them to the other keys.

CD Track
38

Combining Natural Minor & Minor Pentatonic Scales

When improvising you combine different scales to create unique phrasings. A common combination is the natural minor and minor pentatonic scales. Play each natural minor scale position and make a note to where the minor pentatonic scales are inside these positions. Look at the first two positions in the key of "B" below:

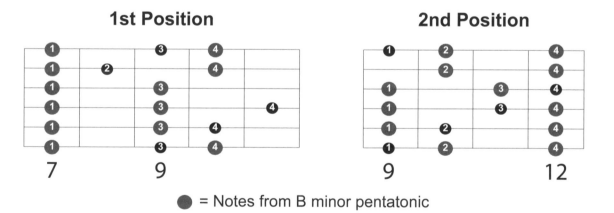

● = Notes from B minor pentatonic

Now over the "Minor Seventh Chord Progression" full band backing track improvise with both of these scales. Play one phrase with the natural minor and the next with the minor pentatonic scales back and forth in a talk back fashion. I've included an example to get you started:

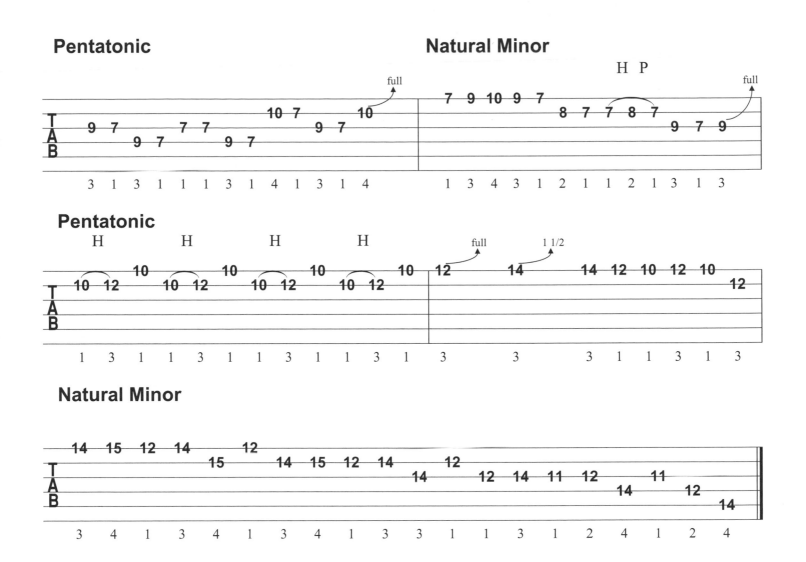

Pentatonic

Natural Minor

Pentatonic

Natural Minor

Major Scale Circle of 5th's

The Sharped Major Keys

Now it's time to learn the circle of 5ths. Starting with the key of "C" you can find the next scale in key signature order by going to the 5th degree. This is called the circle of 5ths and you will use this to practice the major scales that have sharps within them. You are going to use a one octave major scale pattern to play through the exercise. If you notice, from one major scale to the next you are adding one sharped note to the scale. Practicing them this way not only strengthens your ability to play the scales, it will also help you to remember the order in which the scales follow in key signature order. Play through all of the following patterns:

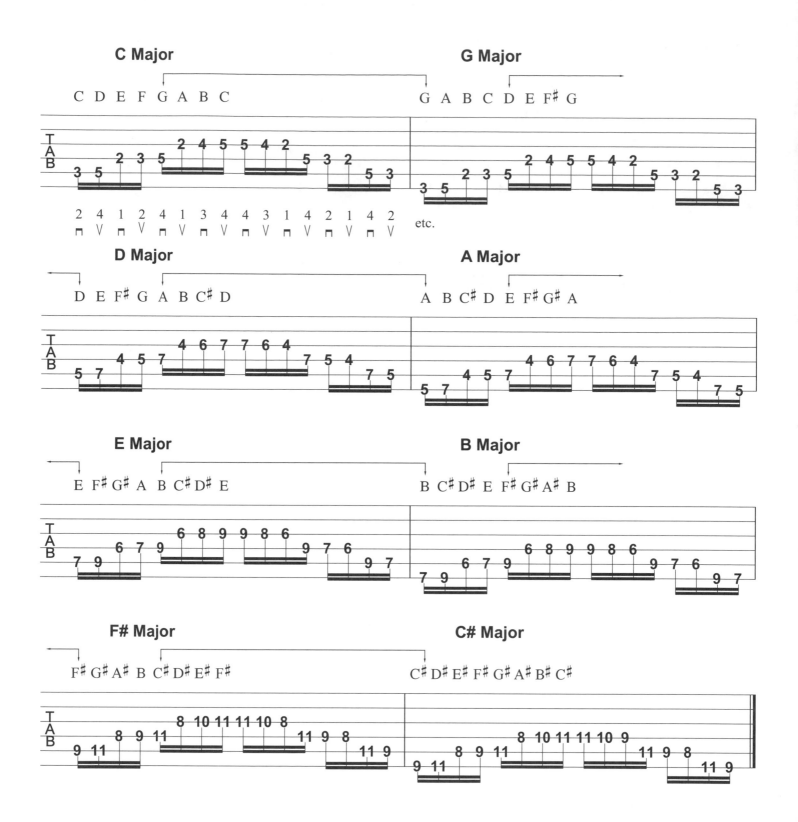

MUSIC ASSIGNMENT

As you play each pattern, say out loud the name of each note. At the end of each, say the key name and the sharps that are included. Here's an example, if you were playing the key of "A" you would say out loud A – B – C♯ – D – E – F♯ – G♯ than at the end say " The key of "A" has three sharps F♯ – C♯ – G♯." This will help you to commit these scales into memory. I recommend that you write out on paper the notes of each scale you went through in this lesson. Writing these will help you memorize them and also give you a nice list of the scales for your reference.

Arpeggios

Here are some challenging arpeggio examples. Arpeggios don't always have to be played in one position. The first example moves laterally up the neck through an A minor arpeggio. Example 2 is another A minor arpeggio that incorporates a right hand tap of the A root note in the 17th fret. Play through these slow and steady first before speeding up the tempo:

Example 1

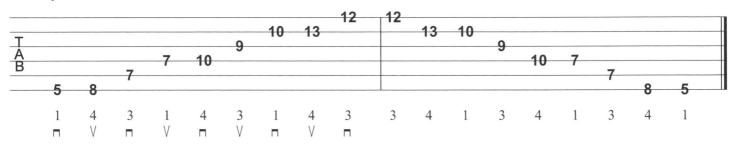

Example 2

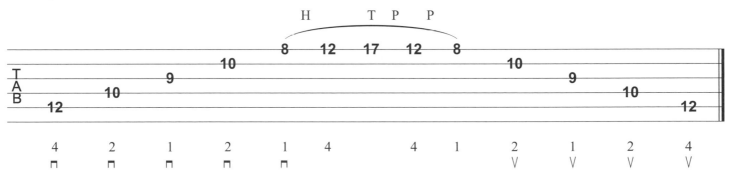

MUSIC ASSIGNMENT

Apply new concepts and create your own variations. For example, one arpeggio example in this lesson incorporated a right hand tap. Learn this example then take the concept of tapping within an arpeggio and apply it to another arpeggio you know. Below is another example of how to expand on this concept:

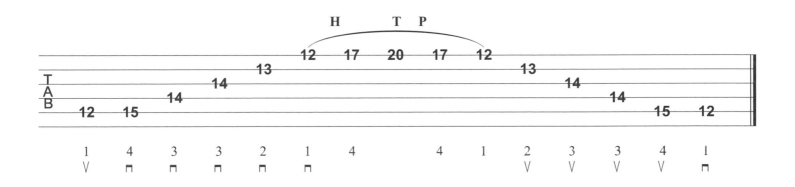

The CAGED System

Chord Shapes and Major Scales

The CAGED system also helps us with playing the major scales. As you have seen in Book 2 with the CAGED system it's quite easy to find the chord tones anywhere on the neck as long as you can quickly find the root notes on the guitar strings.

When you learn the major scale positions for the guitar it's a lot to remember. This gets even harder when you have to think about these positions in twelve different keys. By combining the major scales with the CAGED sequence of chords this task becomes much easier.

By getting used to the relationship between the chords and the scales you will start to realize that remembering these scale positions and being able to find them in any key becomes a lot easier. Study the diagrams below and practice playing with these chord shapes and scales across the fretboard. It might seem like a lot of work at first, but you will get used to it quickly:

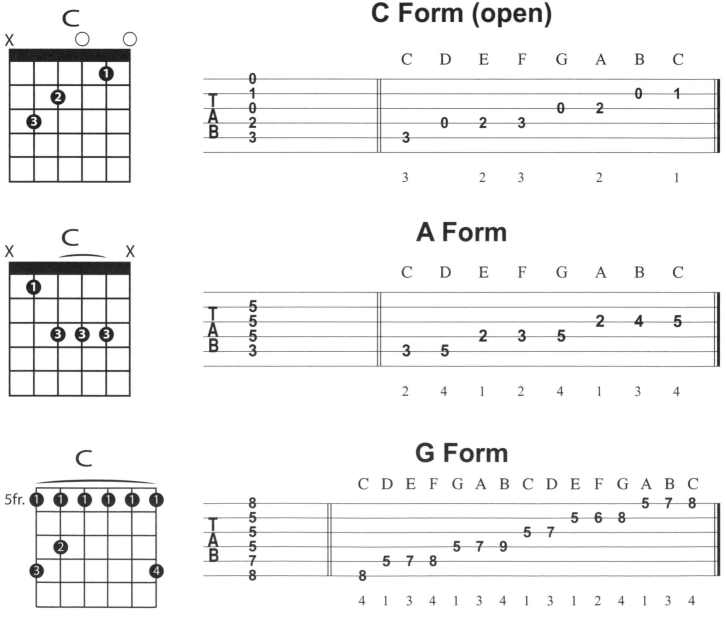

E Form

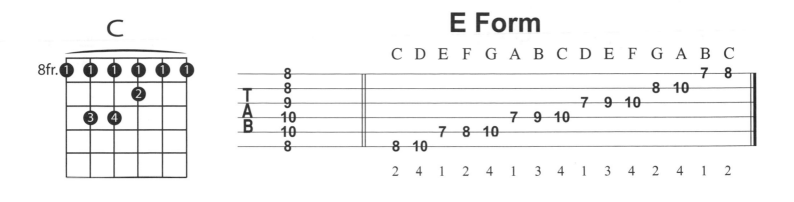

C	D	E	F	G	A	B	C	D	E	F	G	A	B	C

```
      8                                                      7  8
      8                                              8  10
T     9                                      7  9  10
A    10                          7  9  10
B    10              7  8  10
      8           8  10
```

2 4 1 2 4 1 3 4 1 3 4 2 4 1 2

D Form

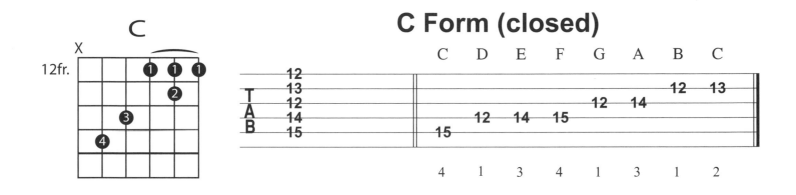

C	D	E	F	G	A	B	C

```
      12
      13                              10  12  13
T     12              9  10  12
A     10      10  12
B
```

2 4 1 2 4 1 3 4

C Form (closed)

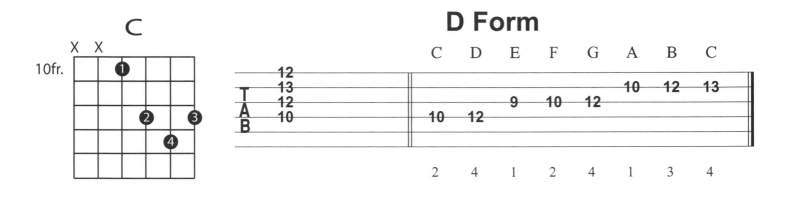

C	D	E	F	G	A	B	C

```
      12
      13                          12  13
T     12              12  14
A     14      12  14  15
B     15      15
```

4 1 3 4 1 3 1 2

MUSIC ASSIGNMENT

Below are the five CAGED chord shapes with E root notes. Apply the scale position you just learned that correspond with each of these chord shapes for the key of "E."

E Major Chords

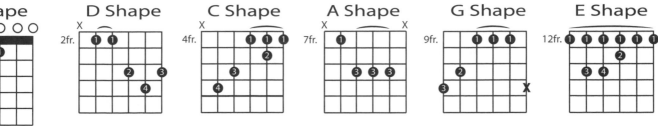

E Shape   D Shape   C Shape   A Shape   G Shape   E Shape

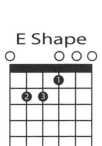

3 String Scale Patterns

SCALE PROFESSOR

The first three strings of a scale are used often when playing leads and melodies. In this lesson you will play a natural minor and pentatonic scale pattern in the key of "A" up the entire fret board using only the first three strings. This is a great exercise to help you learn these scales across the neck. Pay close attention to the fingering as you shift scale positions there are a few tricky spots.

Example 1 A Natural Minor

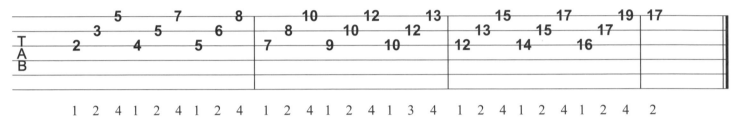

1 2 4 1 2 4 1 2 4 1 2 4 1 2 4 1 3 4 1 2 4 1 2 4 1 2 4 2

Example 2 A Pentatonic

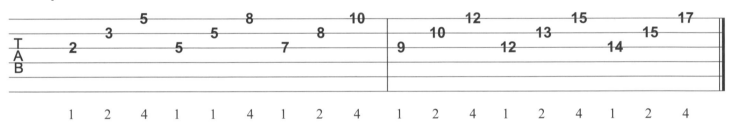

1 2 4 1 1 4 1 2 4 1 2 4 1 2 4 1 2 4

MUSIC ASSIGNMENT

Now take this same pattern and apply it up the 2nd, 3rd and 4th strings. Below is this pattern applies to the natural minor scales. Once you feel comfortable playing this pattern transpose it to the pentatonic scale notes up these same three strings. Pay close attention to the fingering and build your speed up gradually.

Natural Minor

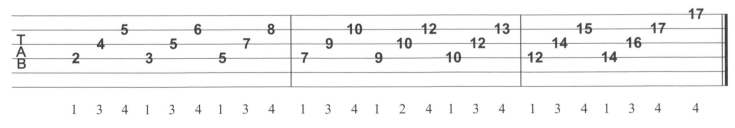

1 3 4 1 3 4 1 3 4 1 3 4 1 2 4 1 3 4 1 3 4 1 3 4 4

Suspended Chords

CHORD PROFESSOR

You've probably seen "sus" after a chord name on sheet music or tab. Sus is an abbreviation for "suspended," it refers to chords that don't follow the common triad pattern. Sus chords commonly replace major or minor chords because they omit the 3rd degree of the chord. There are two commonly used types of suspended chords:

Sus4 – A sus4 chord replaces the 1 – 3 – 5 pattern with 1 – 4 – 5, meaning the 3rd degree (note) is replaced by the 4th. For example to play a Dsus4 chord, instead of playing D – F$\sharp$ – A the 1 – 3 – 5 or major chord formula the Dsus4 chord is D – G – A or the 1 – 4 – 5. Below are some commonly used sus4 chords:

Csus^4

Dsus^4

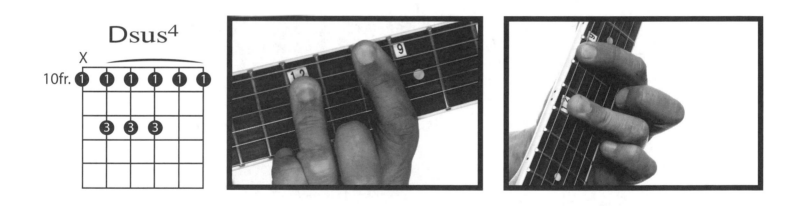

Esus^4

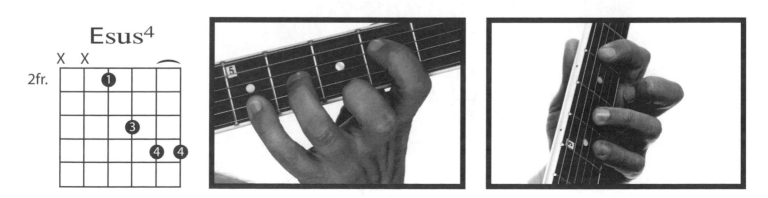

Sus2 – The sus2 chord follows the pattern 1 – 2 – 5, a sus2 chord replaces the 3rd with the 2nd. For example a Dsus2 chord is D – E – A. Below are some commonly used sus2 chords:

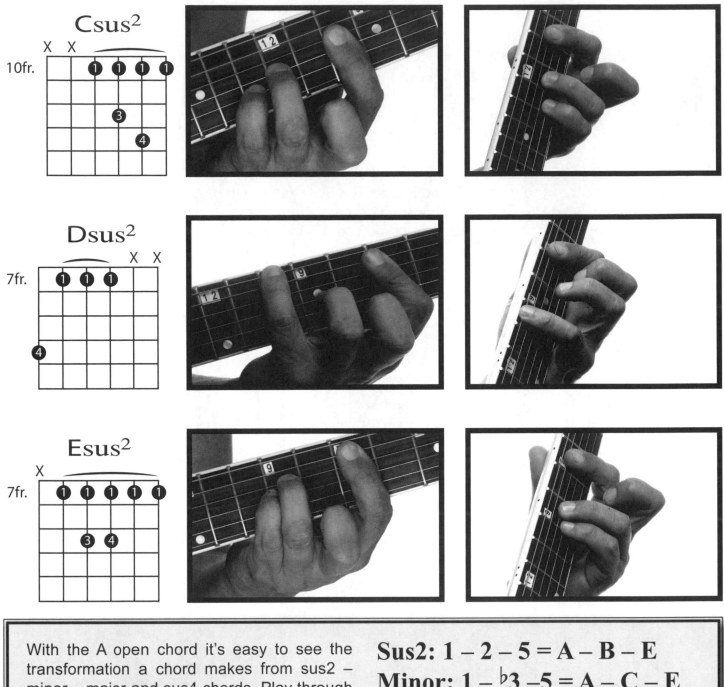

With the A open chord it's easy to see the transformation a chord makes from sus2 – minor – major and sus4 chords. Play through the A chord types below and see how by just changing one note these chords take on a whole new sound.

Sus2: 1 – 2 – 5 = A – B – E
Minor: 1 – ♭3 – 5 = A – C – E
Major: 1 – 3 – 5 = A – C♯ – E
Sus4: 1 – 4 – 5 = A – D – E

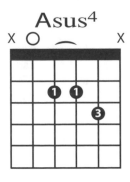

Applying Suspended Chords

In this lesson you will apply suspended chords in a progression. The rhythm for this progression combines strums and single notes. The single notes can be played with a right hand mute to give the progression a dynamic sound. Play the progression with the bass and drum backing track:

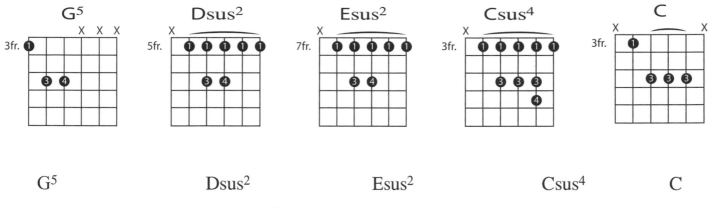

MUSIC ASSIGNMENT

Suspended chords can substitute any major or minor chord. Play some rhythms you have previously learned and substitute suspended chords for some of the major or minor chords. These chords have a unique sound and can add color to a song.

Multi Position Lead Patterns

Natural Minor

Playing lateral lead patterns is a great way to learn to apply your scales in a lead fashion. The two examples in this lesson go through three positions of the natural minor scale in triplet and sixteenth note patterns. Pay close attention to where the pattern shifts to the next scale. You should always slide up on the 4th and 3rd strings with your first finger.

Positions 1-3 Triplets

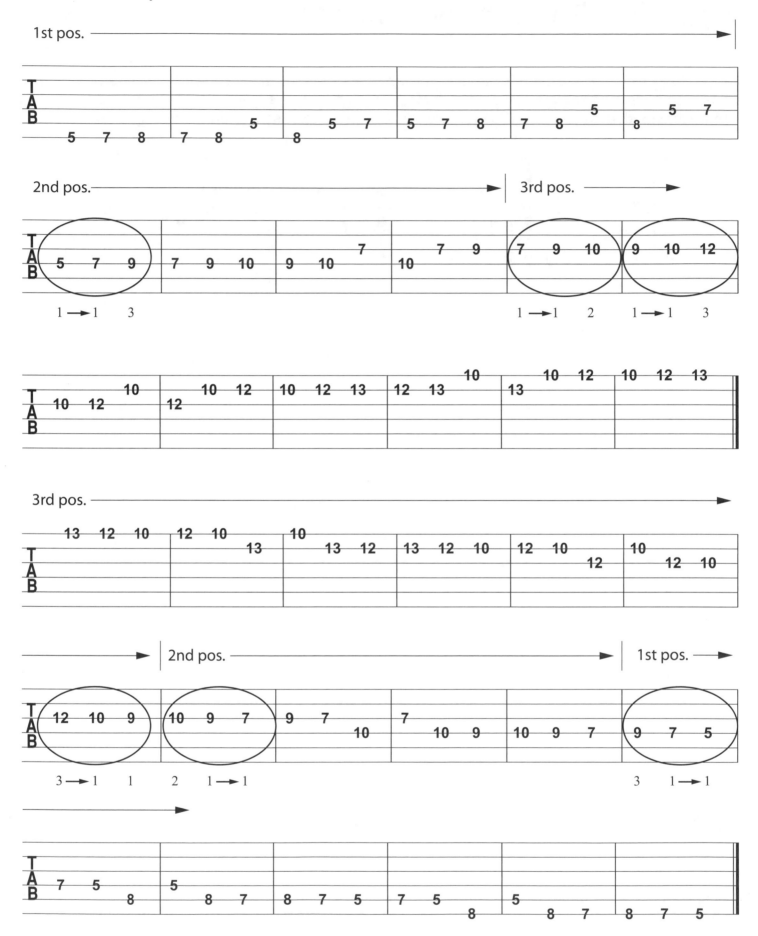

48

Positions 1-3 Sixteenths

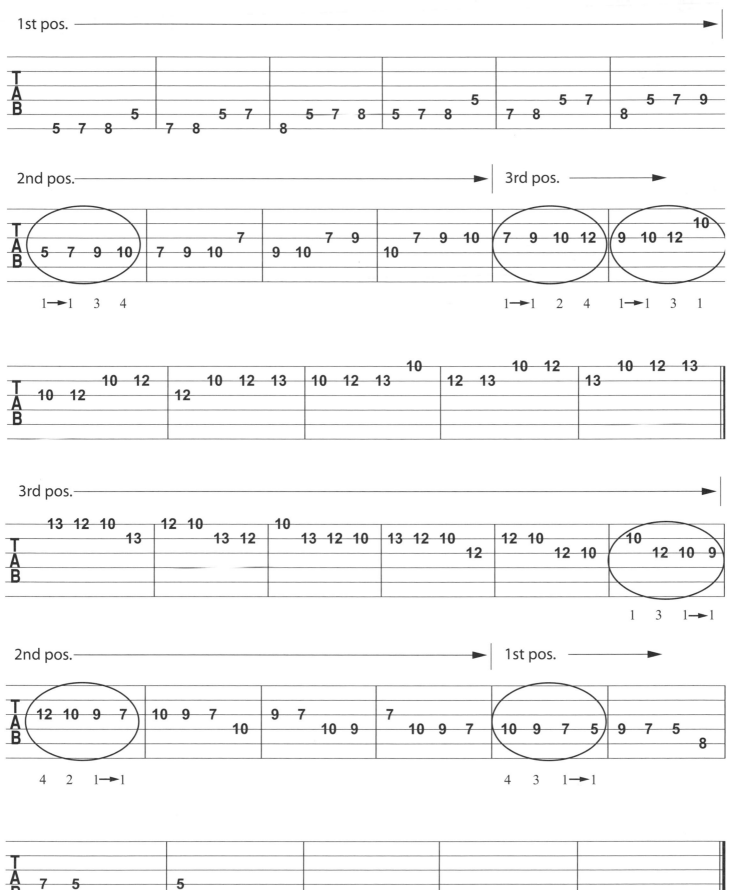

MUSIC ASSIGNMENT

Now play these multi position lead patterns through the 3rd, 4th and 5th natural minor scales. Also transpose these to other keys such as E which is a very popular key.

CD Track
47-48

Riff Challenge #2

Here are a few challenging and fun riffs to spice up your playing. Remember these riffs come directly from your natural minor scales so pay attention to where they are within the position:

Riff #1 A Minor

```
T    6  5        5           5 | 8  6  5      6  5      6 | 5  8  6  5  6  5
A       7  5       7  5          7        7        8          7  5  7
B
```

   2 1 3 1 1 3 1 1   4 2 1 3 2 1 3 2   1 4 2 1 2 1 3 1 3

Riff #2 E Minor

```
                                                                              full
T    5  3  5  3          7  5  7  5          8  7  8  7          10 8 10 8      10
A          5  3             7  5             8  7               10 8
B :                   ::                 ::                 ::                 :
```

   3 1 3 1 3 1   3 1 3 1 3 1   2 1 2 1 2 1   3 1 3 1 3 1   3

Major Scale Circle of 4th's

The Flatted Major Keys

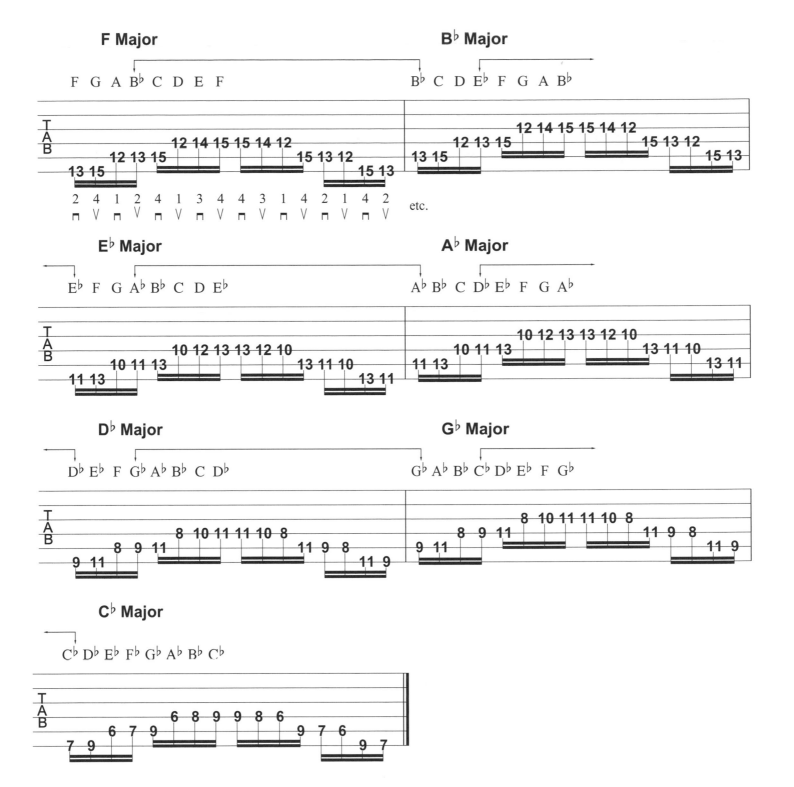

MUSIC ASSIGNMENT

As you did with the circle of 5ths call out the name of each note as you play them. Next write out all seven keys in key signature order.

Get ready for some advanced right hand tapping techniques. These examples will help you see how to add tapping into your lead playing to create unique sounds that you would not be able to attain with standard playing. All these examples come from the natural minor scales in the key of "A." These are very challenging so be patient, they may take practice to master:

Example 1

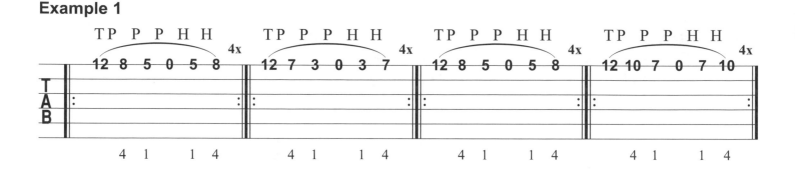

In Examples 2 and 3 continue to use the hammer on and pull off techniques combined with right hand tapping to hear the unique sound of each example.

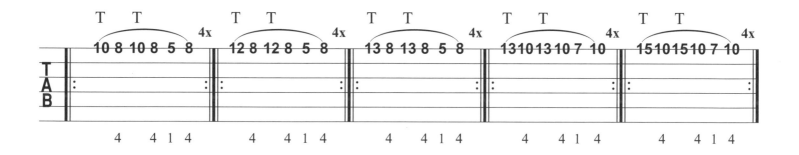

Example 3

 **MUSIC ASSIGNMENT**

The examples use the notes of the natural minor scales in the key of "A" across the 1st string. Transpose the three examples to the 2nd, 3rd, and 4th strings. Make sure to stay within the notes of the scale. You can also vary the patterns to create your own versions.

Intervals

An interval is the distance between two notes. Each interval has a unique sound that you should begin to memorize and train your ear to hear. Intervals are used in chord and scale construction. Learning these intervals will help you understand music and how it is put together. Play through each interval in this lesson and learn their sound:

♩ = Root Note   ♩ = Interval Note

After you get familiar with the sound of each interval go to the *Lesson Support* site and test yourself with the "Ear Trainer" quizzes. By testing yourself you will see which intervals you need to work on to develop a great ear.

Major Pentatonic Scales

SCALE PROFESSOR

Major pentatonic scales are built using the 1 – 2 – 3 – 5 – 6 degrees of the major scale. These scales have their own unique sound and can be used in many applications. The scale patterns will be easy for you to learn because you already know the shapes from the minor pentatonic scales. The thing that will be different is where the root notes are within each scale pattern. The following are the five D major pentatonic scales:

1st Position

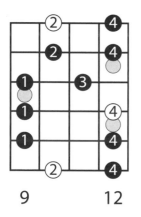

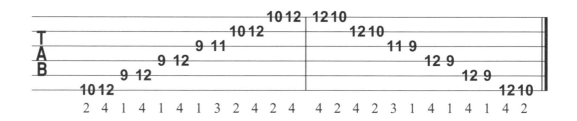

2nd Position

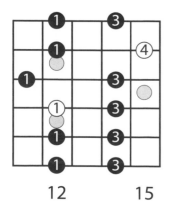

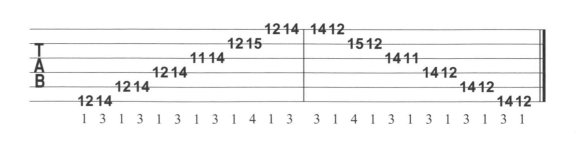

3rd Position

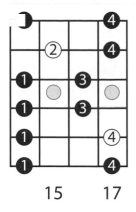

15 17

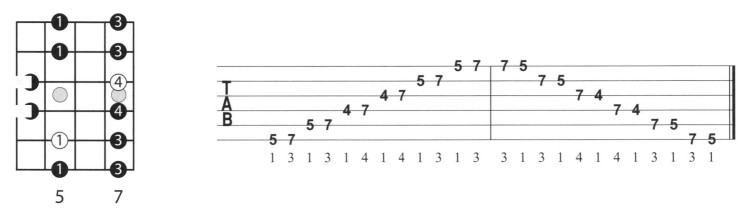

4th Position

5 7

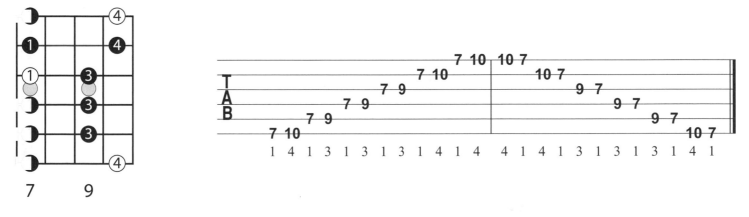

5th Position

7 9

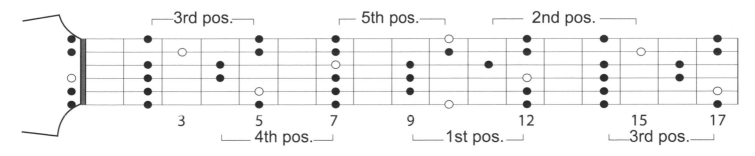

Key of D Major Pentatonic Scales

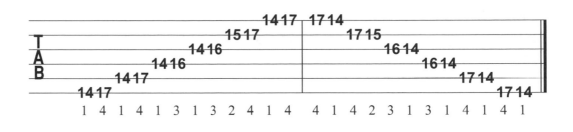

55

The 3 Fret Rule

There is a trick you can use to find a major pentatonic scale quickly. Since you know the minor pentatonic scales you can use them as a reference. Move the minor pentatonic scales in any key down three frets and they will be major pentatonic scales in that same key. I call this the "3 Fret Rule." The first position D minor pentatonic scale starts in the 10th fret, move that scale down three frets to the 7th fret and you have a D major pentatonic scale. Notice how the root notes change within each scale. Look below and see how this works:

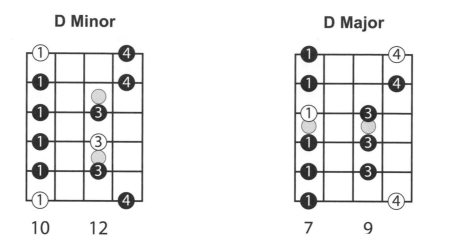

D Minor   10   12

D Major   7   9

Although you know these scale pattern shapes already, the most difficult thing will be to think of them differently and not as minor pentatonic scales. By memorizing where the root notes are within each position you can learn them as major pentatonic scales easier. Play through each position and then play only the root notes, this will give you the tone center sound to help you hear them as major pentatonic scales.

 **MUSIC ASSIGNMENT**

Now take the major pentatonic scales and learn them in the keys of "A" and "E" major. You can start with the minor keys and use the 3 fret rule to change the keys easily. Memorize these keys so you can use them in your lead playing.

A Minor

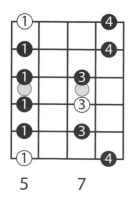

5   7

A Major

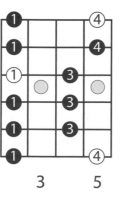

3   5

E Minor

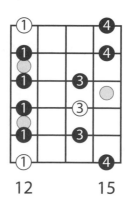

12   15

E Major

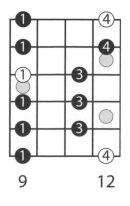

9   12

Applying the Major Pentatonic Scales

Now use the D major pentatonic scales in a creative manner. Let's use a simple major 1 – 5 – 4 – 5 progression to apply the D major pentatonic scales. Many hit songs have been written in all genres of music using this type progression. First play the progression with the bass and drum backing track. Next use the full band backing track and start to make melodies and lead phrasings over it. Keep in mind where the root notes are as you improvise. I have included three riffs to get you started:

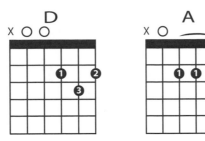
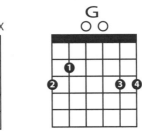

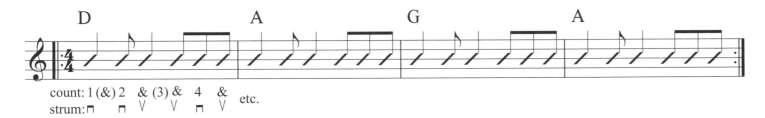

Riff 1

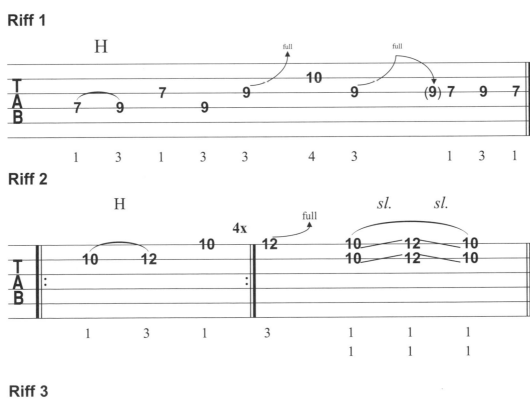

Riff 2

Riff 3

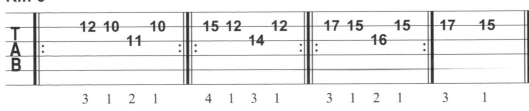

57

Mozart Sonata #11
Rondo Alla Turca

Single string classical pieces are great to learn for a few reasons. First, they are examples of how a great melody is written; they have masterful movement and phrasing. Secondly, they are good finger coordination exercises. This Mozart Sonata is very challenging and will take some time to master. Take this section by section and start very slowly.

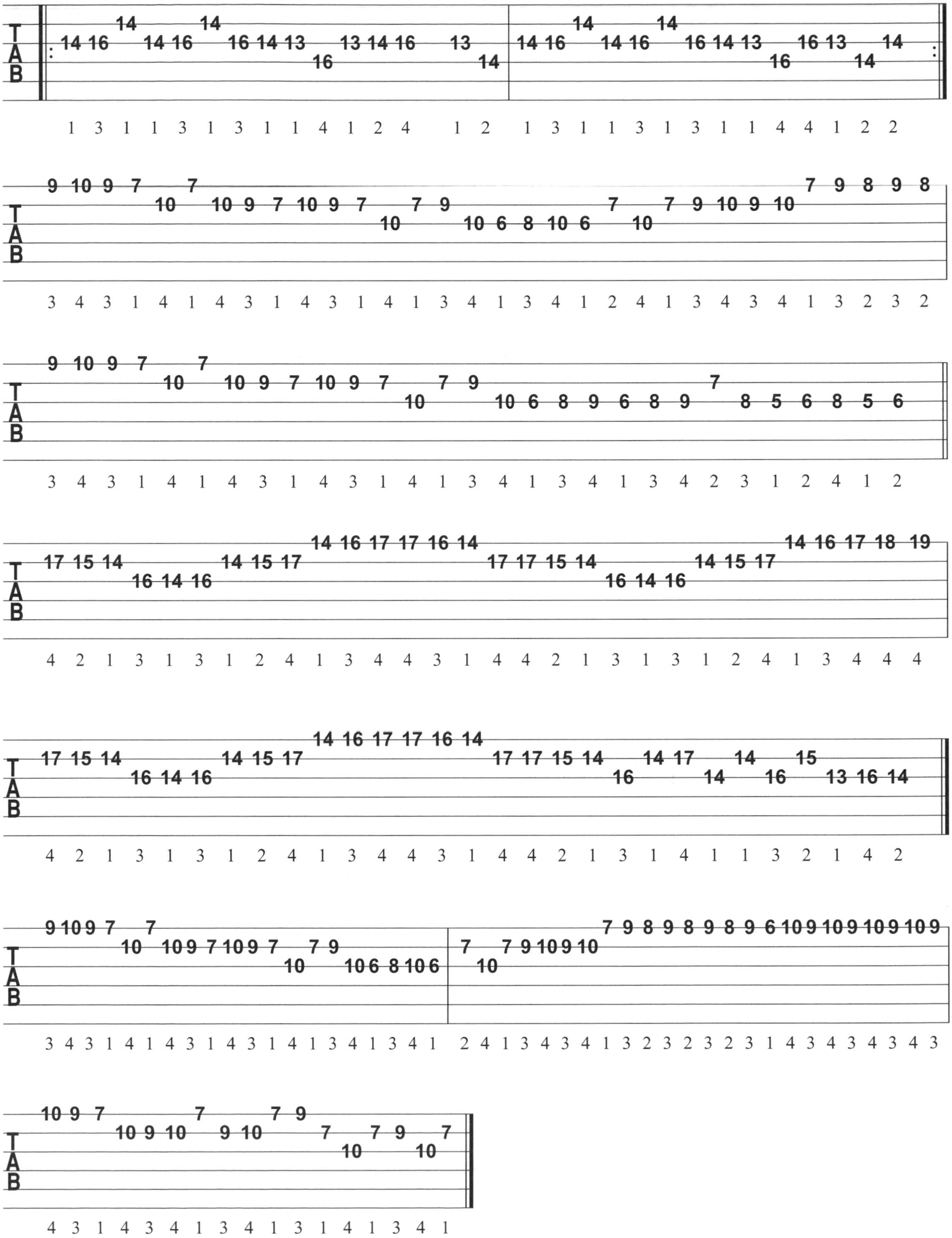

```
System 1 (repeated):
14        14              14        14
14 16  14 16   16 14 13   13 14 16   13      14 16   14 16   16 14 13   16 13   14
                   16                14                            16              14

Fingering: 1 3 1 1 3 1 3 1 1 4 1 2 4   1 2 | 1 3 1 1 3 1 3 1 1 4 4 1 2 2

System 2:
9 10 9 7    7                                                    7 9 8 9 8
        10    10 9 7 10 9 7   7 9              7     7 9 10 9 10
                      10     10 6 8 10 6    10

Fingering: 3 4 3 1 4 1 4 3 1 4 1 3 4 1 3 4 1 2 4 1 3 4 3 4 1 3 2 3 2

System 3:
9 10 9 7    7
        10    10 9 7 10 9 7   7 9                        7
                      10     10 6 8 9 6 8 9    8 5 6 8 5 6

Fingering: 3 4 3 1 4 1 4 3 1 4 3 1 4 1 3 4 1 3 4 2 3 1 2 4 1 2

System 4:
                  14 16 17 17 16 14                              14 16 17 18 19
17 15 14      14 15 17                17 17 15 14      14 15 17
       16 14 16                              16 14 16

Fingering: 4 2 1 3 1 3 1 2 4 1 3 4 4 3 1 4 2 1 3 1 3 1 2 4 1 3 4 4 4

System 5:
                  14 16 17 17 16 14                          14        15
17 15 14      14 15 17                17 17 15 14   14 17
       16 14 16                              16        14        16   13 16 14

Fingering: 4 2 1 3 1 3 1 2 4 1 3 4 4 3 1 4 2 1 3 1 4 1 1 3 2 1 4 2

System 6:
9 10 9 7   7                                      7 9 8 9 8 9 8 9 6 10 9 10 9 10 9 10 9
       10   10 9 7 10 9 7   7 9          7   7 9 10 9 10
                   10     10 6 8 10 6 | 10

Fingering: 3 4 3 1 4 1 4 3 1 4 1 3 4 1 3 4 1 | 2 4 1 3 4 3 4 1 3 2 3 2 3 2 3 1 4 3 4 3 4 3 4 3

System 7:
10 9 7        7        7 9
       10 9 10   9 10      7   7 9   7
               10       10

Fingering: 4 3 1 4 3 4 1 3 4 1 3 1 4 1 3 4 1
```

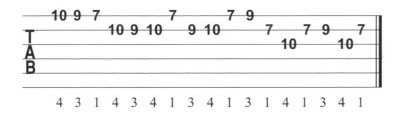

All 15 Major Scales

Now that you have learned all the sharped and flatted keys, you need to make a master chart that includes all 15 major scales. Use the blank scale chart sheet and write out all the scales. Keep this list handy because you will use this to construct chords and create a chord scale for each key that will guide you into song writing.

The Sharp Keys

C Major	C	D	E	F	G	A	B
G Major	G	A	B	C	D	E	F#
D Major							
A Major							
E Major							
B Major							
F# Major							
C# Major							

The Flat Keys

F Major							
B♭ Major							
E♭ Major							
A♭ Major							
D♭ Major							
G♭ Major							
C♭ Major							

Learn Guitar 3 - Quiz 2
Once you complete this section go to RockHouseSchool.com and take the quiz to track your progress. You will receive an email with your results and suggestions.

Creating Melodies & Hooks

It's easy to get stuck in ruts and find it difficult to think of new ideas. This exercise will help you think outside the box. You are going to write a melody without using your guitar and then transpose it to the guitar afterwards. I want you to think like a singer and hum a melody over the major 7th chord progression. By humming you will get new melody ideas you may not have thought by playing on the guitar. Play though the A major scale below to get the note possibilities in your mind, then as the progression backing track is playing, hum a melody. Keep it simple and after you have something created find the notes on your guitar within the scale. I have included a simple melody constructed in this manner to get you started:

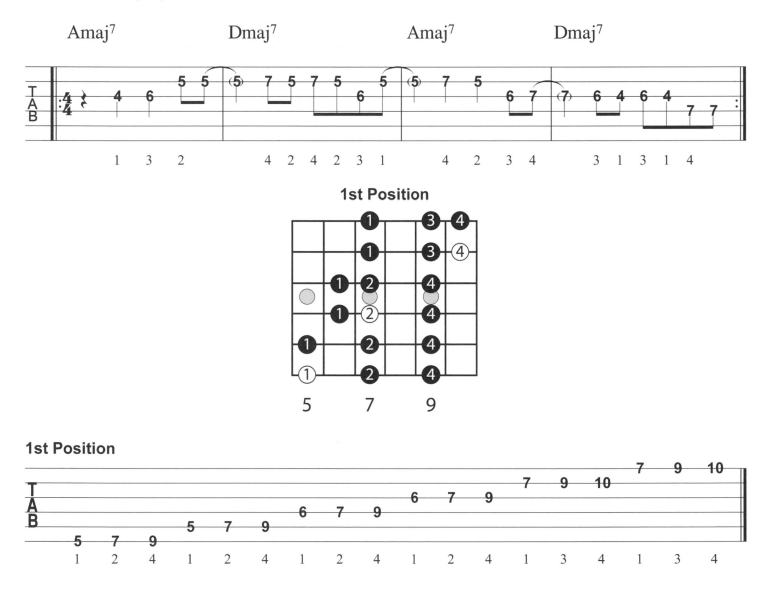

MUSIC ASSIGNMENT

A good way to get used to humming your own melodies is to hum along with melodies of your favorite songs. Also hum along with other instrument solos such as saxophone and piano. Each instrument has unique phrasings that are great when applied to the guitar.

Pivoting

Pivoting is a technique where you go back to a note or series of notes within a phrase. This is a classical technique that sounds great when applied to guitar. Many players use this technique and it is great to add into your "bag of tricks" for lead and rhythm guitar. The following are examples for playing this technique in lead and rhythm applications:

Example 1

E minor

```
12      12      12      12      12      12      12      12
   15      13      12      13      15      13      12      13

 1   4   1   2   1   1   1   2   1   4   1   2   1   1   1   2
 V   ⊓   V   ⊓   V   ⊓   V   ⊓   V   ⊓   V   ⊓   V   ⊓   V   ⊓
```

Example 2

A minor

```
       8       8       8       8       8       8       8       8
    7     5     4                               4       5
                      7       5       7

 3   4   1   4   1   4   3   4   1   4   3   4   1   4   1   4
 ⊓   V   ⊓   V   ⊓   V   ⊓   V   ⊓   V   ⊓   V   ⊓   V   ⊓   V
```

Example 3

G Major

```
    15  12  15      15  12  15      15  12  15      15  12  15
 13              12                              12
                              14              12

 2   4   1   4   1   4   1   4   3   4   1   4   1   4   1   4
 ⊓   V   ⊓   V   ⊓   V   ⊓   V   ⊓   V   ⊓   V   ⊓   V   ⊓   V
```

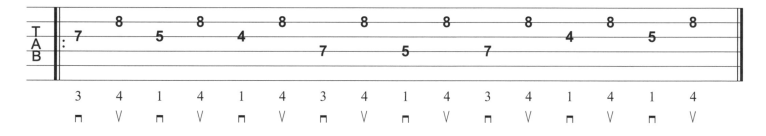

Example 4

A minor

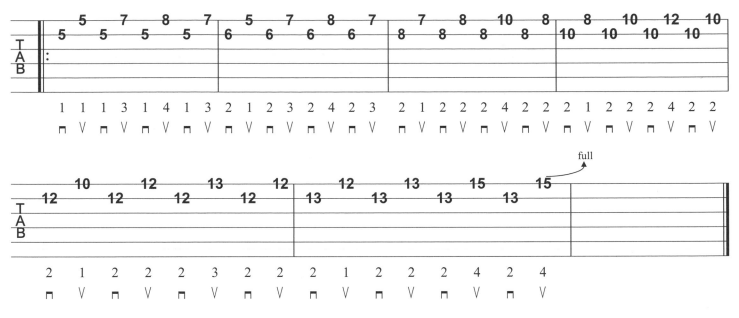

1 1 1 3 1 4 1 3 2 1 2 3 2 4 2 3 2 1 2 2 2 4 2 2 2 1 2 2 2 4 2 2

2 1 2 2 2 3 2 2 2 1 2 2 2 4 2 4

Example 5

E minor

4 2 4 1 4 1 1 2 4 1 4 1 4 1 4 2 4 1 4 1 4 2

Music Assignment

Once you understand the concept of pivoting take the natural minor scales and create some of your own pivot riffs. Remember that you can have a lower note or higher note as a pivot so experiment with each. As always, I recommend that you write down in tab all your ideas and even record them. This will ensure all your ideas last forever.

The BB Box

The BB Box is a series of five notes connecting the 1st and 2nd minor pentatonic scales. Legendary blues guitarist BB King made this famous because of his ability to create masterful leads isolating these notes. The notes can be played with just your first three fingers and this makes it easy to bend and manipulate them. The root note falls right in the middle of these five notes and this allows you to make phrasings up and down effectively. Play through these notes and memorize their location.

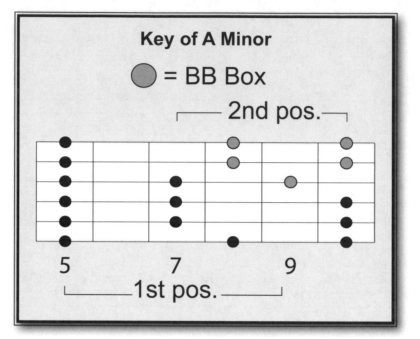

BB Box Notes

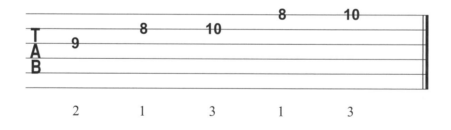

MUSIC ASSIGNMENT

Now it's time to use the BB Box. Over the minor seventh chord progression you learned earlier play the BB Box in the key of "B." This will be two frets higher than the example above.

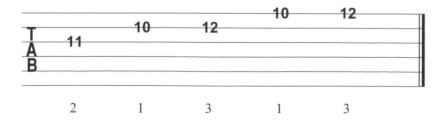

64

9th & 13th Chords

CHORD PROFESSOR

9th and 13th chords are full form chords and are also known as dominant 9th and dominant 13th chords. They are commonly used in jazz and blues music. These two chords have upper extensions that exceed the one octave range. The 9th and 13th degrees are located by counting up a scale as follows $1 - 2 - 3 - 4 - 5 - 6 - 7 - 8 - 9 - 10 - 11 - 12 - 13$.

The chord formula for 9th chords is $1 - 3 - 5 - \flat 7 - 9$. The chord formula for 13th chords is $1 - 3 - 5 - \flat 7 - 13$. Here are some popular fingerings for these chord types:

D^9

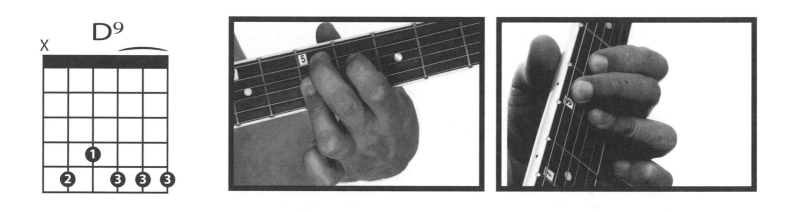

A^9

A^{13}

MUSIC ASSIGNMENT

Transpose these chord fingerings to other keys. Be aware that the root note is also the lowest note in each chord. Next try to make new fingerings using the chord formula. For example, to make an E9th chord you would play the following notes together: E – G♯ – B – D – F♯.

CD Track 60-61

The Jazz Blues Fuse

The jazz blues fuze rhythm is another example of a 12-bar blues progression. This progression uses all 9th chords and is slow, jazzy blues. The rhythm is played with a straight feel in 6/8 time (six-eighth notes per measure). The strumming pattern is indicated above the staff. Count along with the backing track to get the rhythm in your head. The rhythm is eighth note triplets. Next, transpose the blues scale positions to the key of "A" and use them to play leads over the backing track.

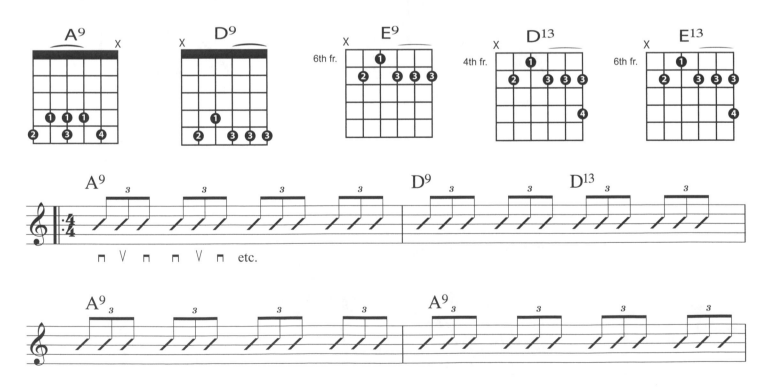

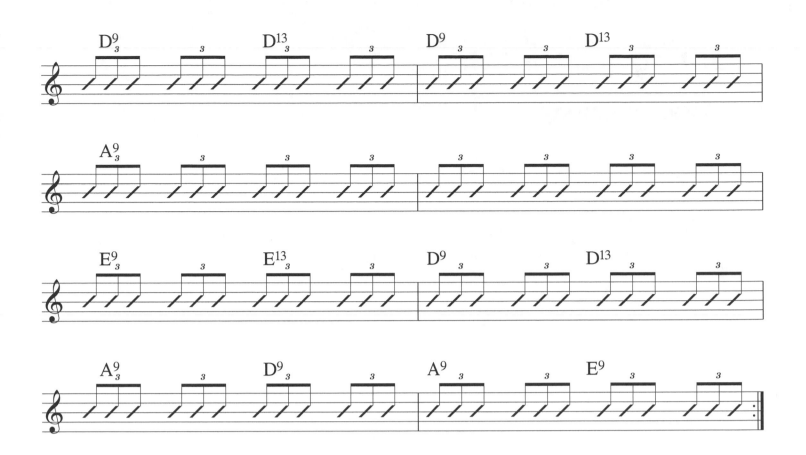

MUSIC ASSIGNMENT

This was a slow tempo rhythm. Change the rhythm to a fast tempo and alter the strum pattern to create a new feel. Follow the example below:

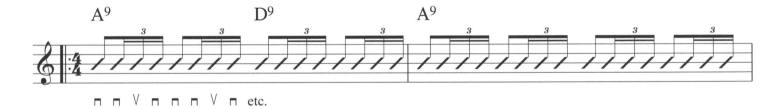

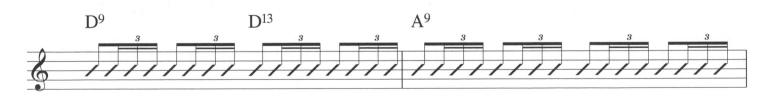

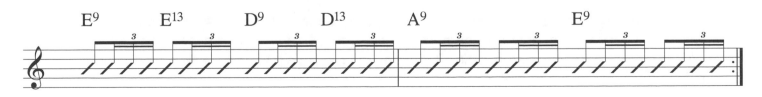

Creating a Chord Scale

2 & 3 Part Harmony

Intervals

Now it's time to put that major scale theory to work and create a chord scale within the key of "C" major. This chord scale will help you see what chords work together within a key and how they can be used to write songs. The first thing we will cover is two part harmony finding the 3rd above each scale tone as follows:

3rd - E - F - G - A - B - C - D - E
ROOT - C - D - E - F - G - A - B - C

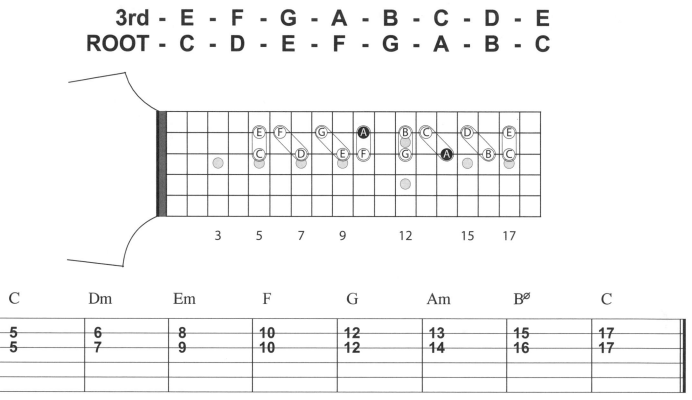

By doing this, you create intervals that tell us what type of chord goes with each degree of the scale. C & E together creates a major interval; D & F make a minor interval because the normal 3rd degree of D would be F♯ so F is a flatted 3rd degree. Doing this to each scale degree would create intervals as follows:

I = major 3rd	ii = minor 3rd	iii = minor 3rd
IV = major 3rd	V = major 3rd	vi = minor 3rd
	vii = minor 3rd	

Now let's add a note, five scale degrees above each of the root notes to create three part harmony or triads. All these notes will be perfect 5ths (P5) or seven half steps up from the root except the 5th above B. The 5th scale tone up from the B note is a diminished 5th (♭5) or 6 half steps up from the root note creating a diminished triad.

Triads

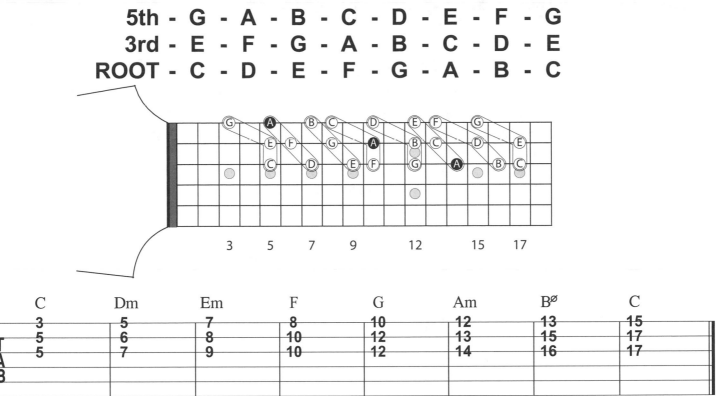

```
5th - G - A - B - C - D - E - F - G
3rd - E - F - G - A - B - C - D - E
ROOT - C - D - E - F - G - A - B - C
```

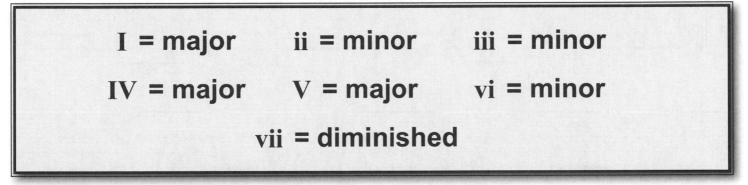

C	Dm	Em	F	G	Am	B∅	C
3	5	7	8	10	12	13	15
5	6	8	10	12	13	15	17
5	7	9	10	12	14	16	17

Adding the 3rd and 5th above each scale degree would create a chord formula that can be applied to any major scale as follows:

I = major	**ii = minor**	**iii = minor**
IV = major	**V = major**	**vi = minor**
	vii = diminished	

So to summarize this, the 1st, 4th and 5th triads will always be major triads. The 2nd, 3rd and 6th triads will always be minor triads. The 7th triad will always be a diminished. This will hold true when applied to any major scale. Below are seven chords in the key of "C" major that can be used to create a song in this key, try to create combinations of these chords to make your own song.

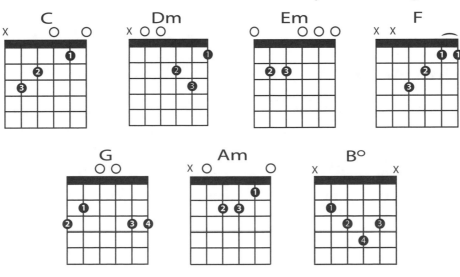

Circle of 4ths Progression in C

CD Track
62-63

The following progression is a slow ballad in the key of "Am." The rhythm is arpeggiated with the notes picked out separately. Finger and hold the chord in each measure and let its notes ring out together. Follow the finger numbers under the tab staff to show you the proper chord fingerings. Play along with the backing track and practice the rhythm's slow ballad feel. The chord change progresses in a pattern of 4ths: the distance from one chord to the next is the interval of a fourth. This is a common change that is also used in many musical styles ranging from classical to metal.

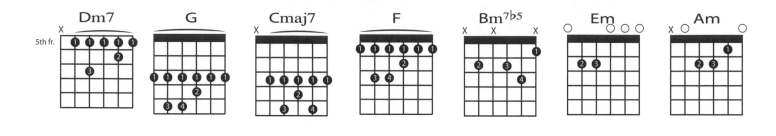

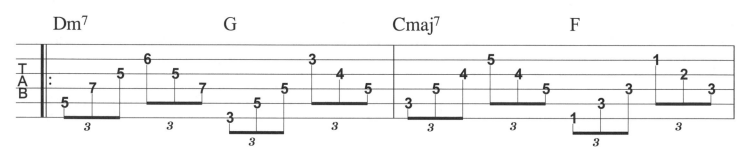

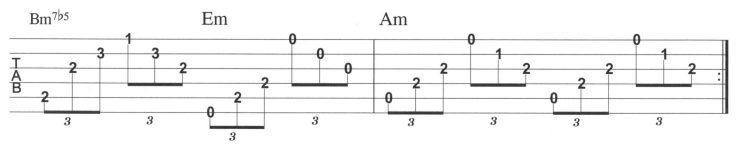

MUSIC ASSIGNMENT

Play the same progression with a strumming pattern. Strum: down – down up down, two times for each chord. Then experiment with other strumming variations. Progressions can be played different ways to get totally different sounds from the same exact chords.

70

Riff Challenge #3

Here are a few more riffs to challenge your fingers. These two riffs are in the key of "A" minor and come directly from the A natural minor scales. Build your speed up slowly.

Riff #1 A minor

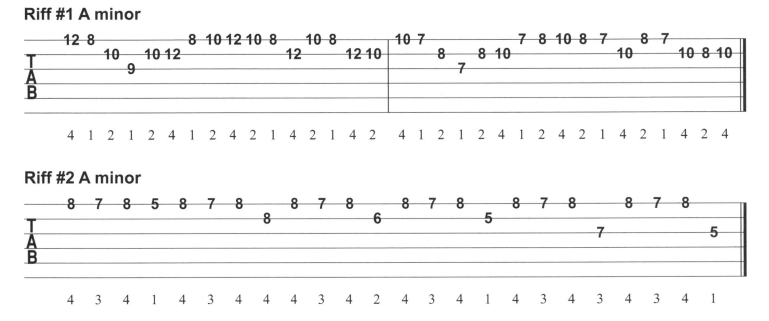

String Skipping Arpeggio Progression

Many great players use string skipping to play arpeggios effectively. Notice that there are pull offs and hammer ons that help to make the notes flow. These arpeggios form a progression that sounds great when played quickly.

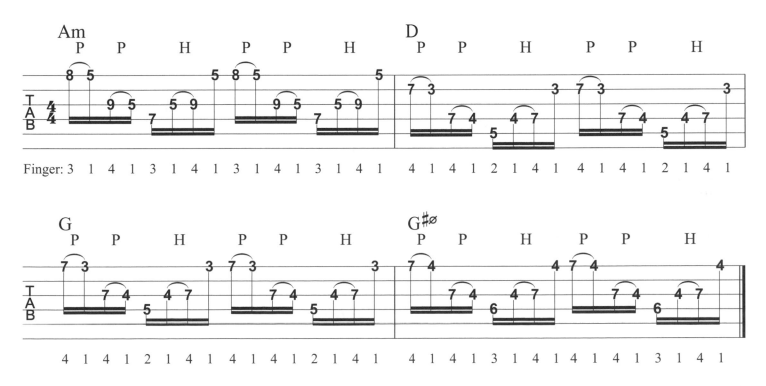

Song Construction

When writing a song there are common sections that you should learn that will help you structure some great songs. The two sections that make the main song structure are the verse and chorus. All the other sections give the song dynamics and diversity. A verse tells the story of a song while the chorus is a repetitive catchy section that seems to brainwash the listeners at times. Below are the most common sections that are used to form songs:

Introduction

The introduction or "intro" is a unique section that comes at the beginning of the song. It usually builds up suspense for the listener. The intro may be based around the chords used in the verse, chorus, or bridge, or main riff of the song.

Verse

The verse tells the story of the song. When two or more sections of the song have the same music with different lyrics these sections are most likely considered the verses. Each verse section can have the same melody and rhythm, it is the lyrics that will vary. Often a verse has a chord structure that is longer before repeating giving more time to tell the story. A song can have many verses.

Pre-Chorus

When a song incorporates a pre-chorus it occurs after the verse and functions to connect the verse to the chorus. Often when the verse and chorus use the same chord structure the pre-chorus will introduce a new section in order to make the chorus have more impact.

Chorus

The chorus or "refrain" is the repetitive catchy section of a song. The chorus often contrasts the verse melody and rhythm to create a higher level of dynamics. When two or more sections of the song have basically, identical music and lyrics, these sections are most likely considered the chorus. A chorus usually has a chord structure that is short and repeats often to give it a catchy effect. A chorus usually has a strong focus on the root chord or the chord that is the name of the key. Sometimes the chorus is repeated at the end and at the beginning of a song.

Bridge

A bridge is a section that connects two parts of a song. The bridge usually differs from the verse and the chorus in its chord structure and lyrics. Unlike a verse or chorus section, a bridge does not always contain lyrics. A bridge may be performed as an instrumental section with a melody.

Lead Section

A lead section or "solo" is a section designed to showcase an instrument. The lead section may take place over the chords from the verse, chorus, or bridge, or over a standard solo backing progression, such as a 12-bar blues progression. In some cases the melody that the singer sang for the chorus is played with embellishments such as bends, scale runs and arpeggios to form a lead section.

Break Down

A break down is a section that lowers the dynamic level to set up a higher dynamic section often the chorus. The break down is usually an instrumental section and often has a build up at the end. In metal music, breakdowns are used to energize the crowd with a heavy, rhythmic section.

Outro

An outro is a short ending section to the song. Often the outro is the chorus of the song repeated with layered vocal and instrumental melodies called the "chorus out."

Common Song Structures

There are hundreds of different possible combinations of these song sections that have been used to create songs. Here are a few common structures using the core sections verse, chorus and bridge. The other sections are usually added around these for variations.

Verse - Verse - Chorus - Verse - Chorus	A - A - B - A - B
Verse - Chorus - Verse - Chorus - Verse - Chorus	A - B - A - B - A - B
Verse - Verse - Verse	A - A - A
Verse - Chorus - Verse - Chorus - Bridge - Chorus	A - B - A - B - C - B

MUSIC ASSIGNMENT

To fully understand how these sections are used to construct songs lets analyze some songs. Pick a group of 10 of your favorite songs. As the song is playing write the structure of each song out on paper. By doing this you will be able to see and hear how songs are put together.

Chordal Soloing Exercise

Chordal soloing is a technique that has several ways to be applied. One way would be to follow the chords of a progression and change keys for each chord. For example, if the progression went from Am to F you would play the A natural minor scale over the Am chord and the F major scale over the F chord.

The second way (which we will go through in this lesson) is to follow the chords within one key or scale. So if you had that same Am to F progression you would play the A natural minor scale over the Am chord and for the F chord you would still play the A natural minor scale; but, you would target the F note within the scale as the tone center. By beginning or ending your riffs and phrasings on the root note you get a strong sense of the tone center. Below is an example of this chordal soloing technique:

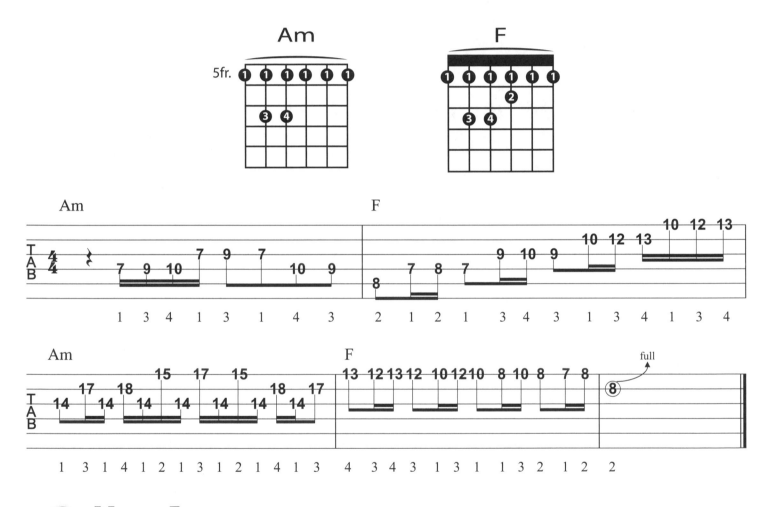

MUSIC ASSIGNMENT

Now it's your turn to create a solo using this technique. Use the full band backing track and follow the chord changes within the natural minor scale. Your target notes will be A over the Am chord and F over the F chord. By starting or ending your phrasings on the root notes of each chord you create a strong tonal center and chordal soloing effect.

Diatonic 3rd Harmony

Adding a harmony will enhance a melody and make it stand out. Let's create a harmony lead section in diatonic 3rds. You learned the basics of how to find a diatonic 3rd within a major scale in the Creating a Chord Scale lesson, now let's apply this to creating a lead. Diatonic means relating to the scale or key. For diatonic 3rds you will add a note three scale degrees above each melody note directly from the same scale. To start, we are going to use the C major 1st position scale and create a melody line. Below see a melody created directly from this scale:

Root

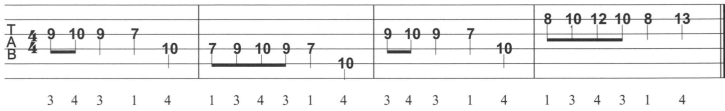

To create a harmony in diatonic 3rds take each note and find the note three scale degrees above it within the C major scale. For example for C, go up three scale degrees C – D – E and E will be the harmony note. Below is the complete harmony that corresponds to the melody above:

Diatonic 3rds

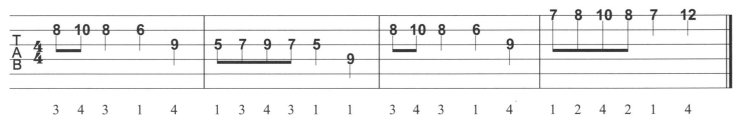

Now play both parts together to hear the diatonic 3rd harmony:

Root and Diatonic 3rds Together

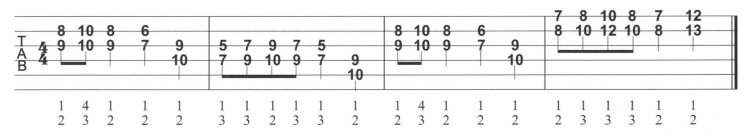

Music Assignment

Take the A natural minor scale and write a melody and harmony in thirds. First, start with the melody line, make it simple because it will be easier to create the harmony. Write the melody on a sheet of tab. Next take each note and find the note three scale degrees above it and write that on the sheet of tab as well. After you have it finished write them together in tab and play the complete harmony.

Blues Riff Rhythm

CD Track
73-74

This is a single note riff rhythm in E. After you learn the rhythm, you can solo over the backing track using the E blues scales and all of the techniques you've learned. The progression is based on a I – IV – V, 12-bar blues progression; the chord names above the tab staff are there as a reference to outline the basic harmony.

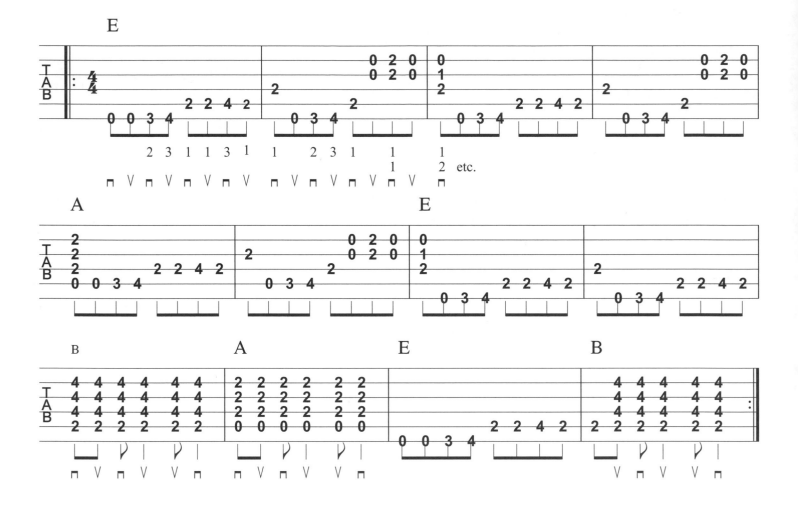

MUSIC ASSIGNMENT

Now play this blues rhythm using the shuffle feel. Adding the shuffle feel to this rhythm will give it a bouncy blues feel.

Blues Lead Key of "E"

After you learn this lead, create your own and work on your improvisational skills using all of the techniques you've learned. This lead should be played over the Blues Riff Rhythm from the previous lesson.

77

Call & Response Technique

You can create a call and response effect by switching back and forth between major and minor pentatonic scales while soloing. This is a common technique in blues soloing. In this lesson you will use the major and minor pentatonic scales in the key of "A" in a call and response fashion. I've outlined two scale positions below to use for this exercise. The finger patterns for both scales will be the same; the difference is in the placement of the root notes. Play one phrase in the major scale then the next in the minor back and forth. When done properly it sounds almost like to players having a musical conversation. Play the example below that demonstrates how this technique works:

A Minor

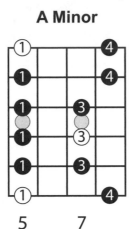

A Major

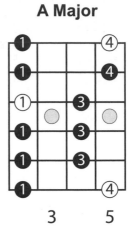

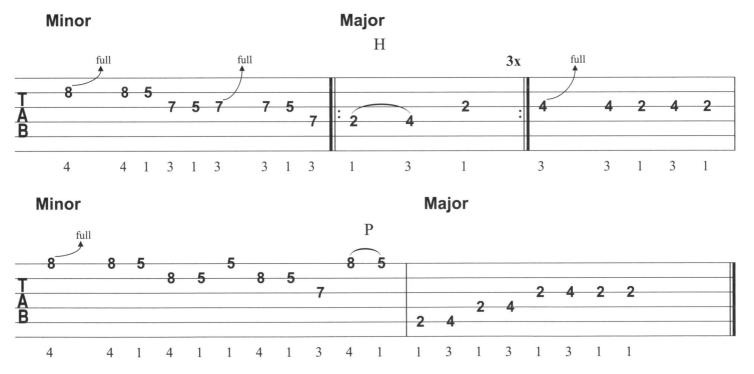

Solo over the Jazz Blues Fuze full band backing track using both the major and minor pentatonic scales. Play for a few bars in major, and then move three frets higher and play in minor for a few bars to achieve a call and response effect.

Pick & Finger Technique

This technique is especially popular with blues and country players. Hold the pick as you normally would, then use your middle and ring fingers to pick additional notes. You can achieve quick jumps from low to high notes using this technique. In the first example, the notes are played together by down picking with the pick and simultaneously plucking upward with the middle finger. Use a pinching motion with the pick and middle finger to pluck the notes together. The left hand fingering is indicated under the staff. Leave your first finger barred across the first three strings while reaching with your third and fourth fingers for the other notes along the 3rd string. Once you get the idea, try coming up with your own riffs and incorporate this style into your improvisational repertoire.

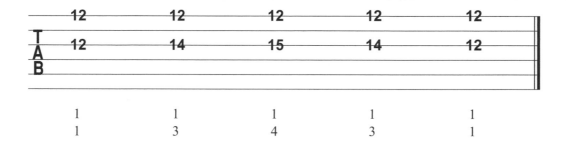

Here are few more examples using the pick and finger technique. The notes in these examples are picked individually, alternating between the pick and middle finger. After you have this technique down, try to use it in different scale positions and keys.

Example 1

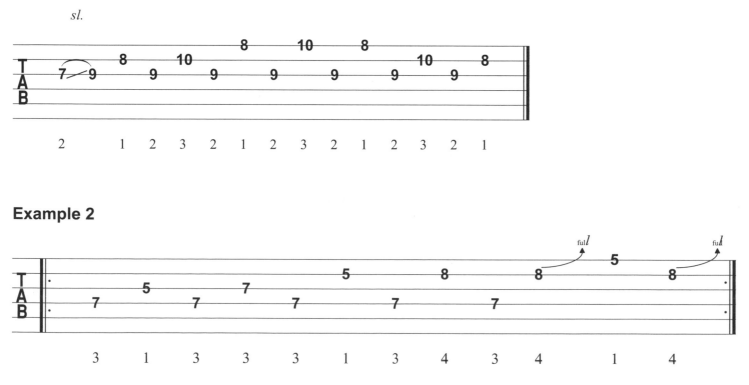

Example 2

Beethoven "Für Elise"

Here is another challenging single string classical piece Beethoven's "Fur Elise." This sounds great when played with distortion. I've also included a version that is more applicable to acoustic guitar. You will need to use the pick and finger technique to play either version. Learn them in sections. Start at a steady slow tempo and build speed gradually.

Electric Version

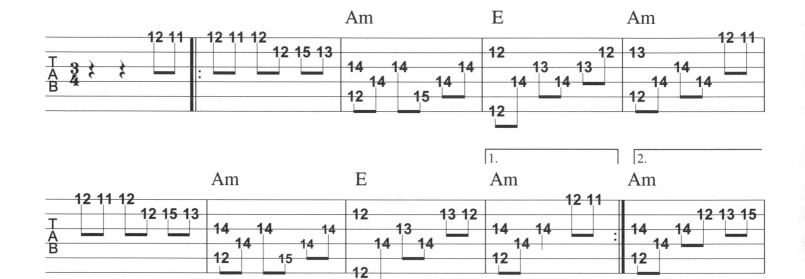

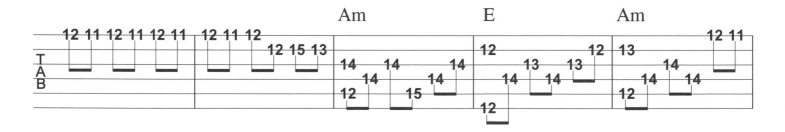

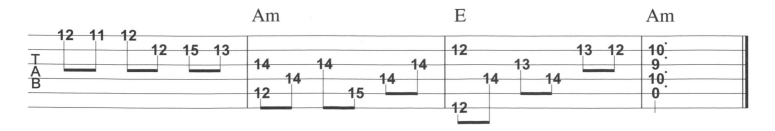

Acoustic Version

As you play this song fret the chord above the staff and pick the notes within.

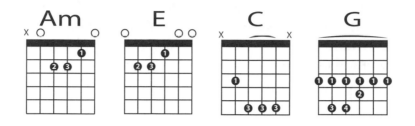

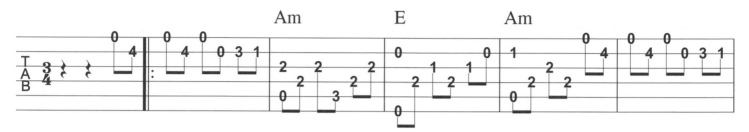

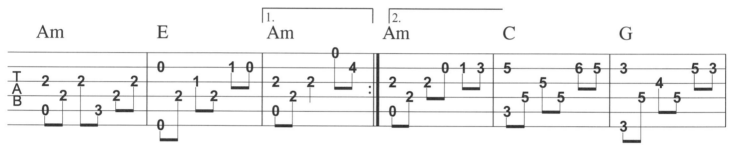

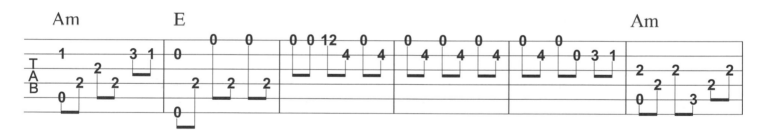

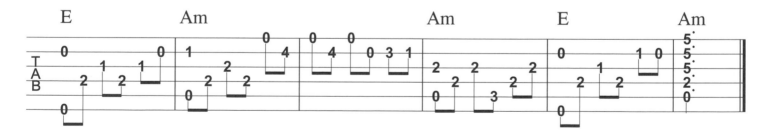

81

Bi-Dextral Scale Hammer Ons

A great way to play two minor pentatonic scales at the same time is to use bi-dextral hammer-ons. In this lesson you will connect the first two scales together. Your left hand with fret the notes of the 1st position scale and your right hand will tap the second note of the 2nd position. Notice how the middle note on each string is a common note that these two scales share.

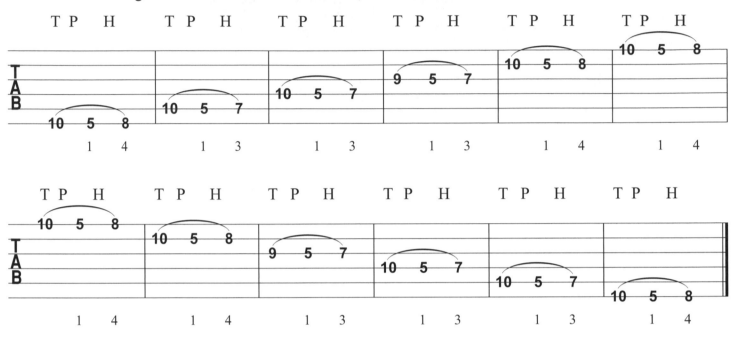

Riff Challenge #4

Here are a few more challenging and fun riffs. These riffs come directly from the C major scales. Pay close attention to where the C root notes are within each example. These notes give the riff a tonal center.

Riff #1

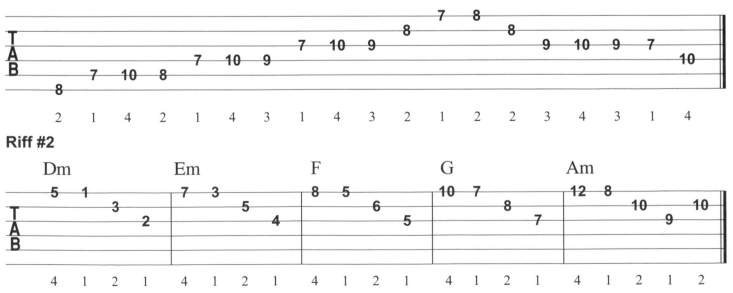

Riff #2

Slapping Technique

While playing finger style (without a pick), you can add a percussive, rhythmic feel to a chord progression by slapping the strings with your thumb. In the exercise below, fret the G chord in the first measure and follow the p-i-m-a right hand fingering, paying attention to where the rhythmic slaps occur in the progression:

Example 1

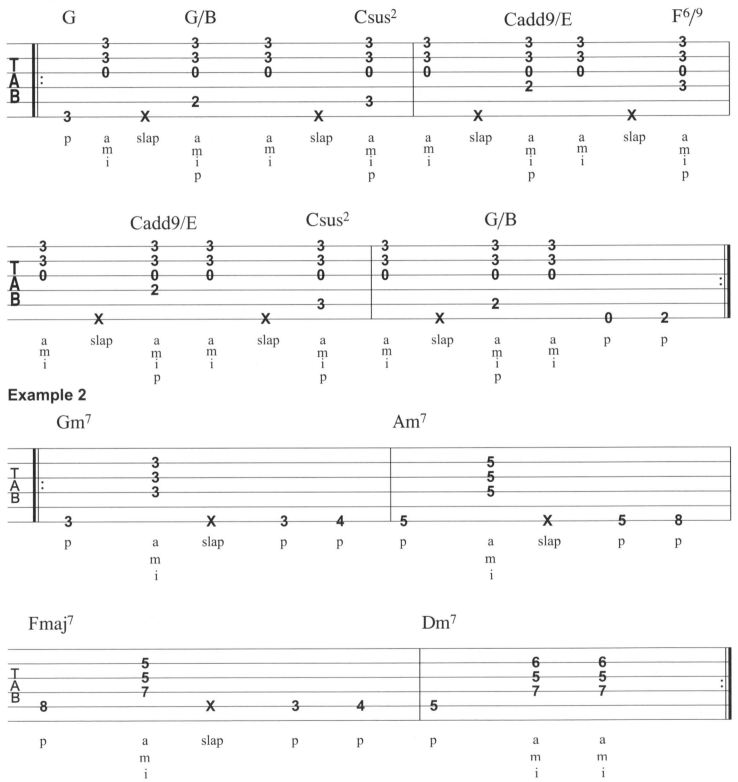

Example 2

Basic Modal Theory

Natural modes are seven note subdivisions of the major scale. Modes are also cousins of the major scale. There are seven diatonic modes within each major scale, but you only have five to learn. The major scale and the minor scale we covered already are two of the seven modes. The major scale is also called the Ionian mode, and the minor scale is also known as the Aeolian mode.

Modes are created by taking any degree of the scale and making it your tone center and playing through the scale notes until you get back to the note you started on. For example, in C major, the notes are C – D – E – F – G – A – B – C. If you started on this scale from the second note D and go back up to D it would be D – E – F – G – A – B – C – D or better known as the D Dorian mode. In this same fashion you can create modes from every scale degree. There are seven natural modes derived from the major scale and they are: Ionian (Major Scale), Dorian, Phrygian, Lydian, Mixolydian, Aeolian (minor Scale) and Locrian.

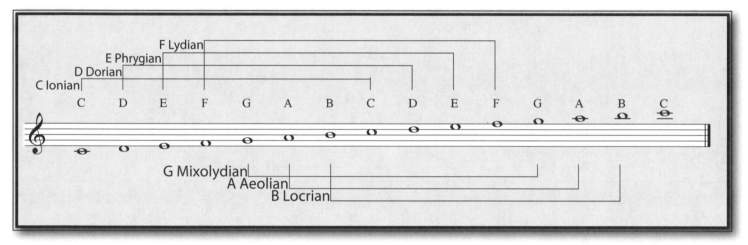

The modes all have names of ancient Greek tribes whose music was originally associated with the distinct sounds of each mode (i.e. Lydian derives from Lydia, etc.). Each mode will have its own tonal quality (happy & sad) because of where the whole and half steps fall within each scale pattern. Each of the modes has its own characteristics much like the different colors on a painter's pallet. As musicians, we paint with sounds as our medium. Understanding the derived modes of the major scale now, will help you later on with chord construction and give you a deeper understanding of how these modes work with chords.

Here are the seven modes derived from the first position major scale pattern:

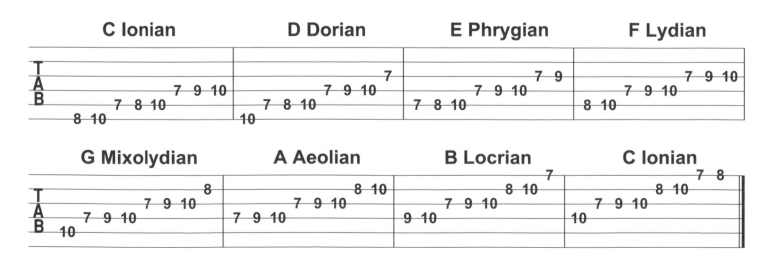

Harmonic Minor &
Phrygian Major Scales

Harmonic Minor

The harmonic minor scale is a sister to the natural minor scale. To form a harmonic minor scale you sharp the seventh degree of the natural minor scale. This creates a 1 ½ step interval between the 6th and 7th degrees. This scale is commonly found in Middle Eastern music.

A natural minor scale A – B – C – D – E – F – G
A harmonic minor scale A – B – C – D – E – F – G#

Below are the first two positions of this scale:

1st Position

2nd Position

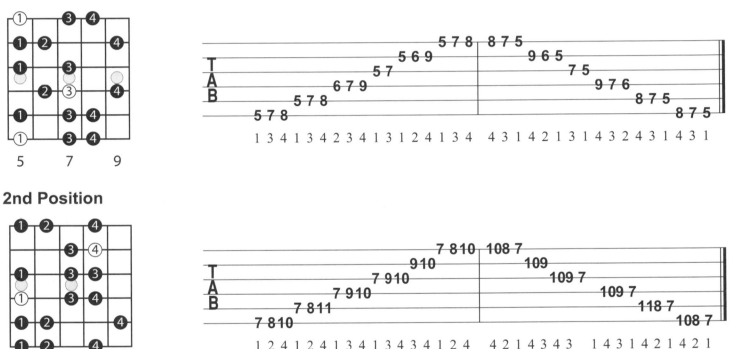

Phrygian Major

As with the major scale the harmonic minor scale can be arranged in modes whose names are based on modified forms of other scales. There is one mode that is commonly used by many guitarists the "Phrygian major." The Phrygian major scale has a few different aliases, it's also known as the Phrygian dominant, Spanish Phrygian, Spanish gypsy and even the Ahava Rabboh. Many players confuse this scale as harmonic minor but it is actually the fifth mode of the harmonic minor scale. Players such as Ritchie Blackmore and Yngwie Malmsteen have used this scale as a staple of their sound. I'm also going to show you these scales across the neck and explain how to apply them over a chord progression. This scale is unusual because the interval between the second and third degrees is an augmented second or 1 1/2 steps; this large interval gives the scale a unique sound like the harmonic minor scale. The sequence of steps that create the Phrygian major scale are: half – augmented – half – whole – half – whole – whole. When related to the degrees of the major scale, it reads like this:

E Phrygian Major: E - F - G# - A - B - C - D - E
1 ♭2 3 4 5 ♭6 ♭7 8

Below find the Phrygian major scales in the key of "E." Play through each position and get the sound of these scales in your ears. Notice that they have quite a distinct sound.

1st Position

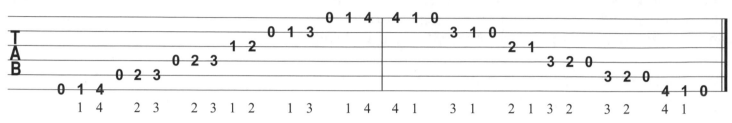

2nd Position

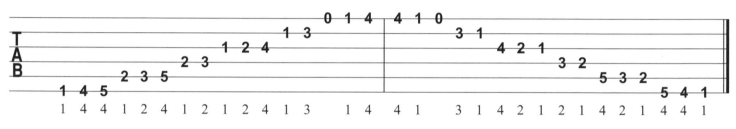

3rd Position

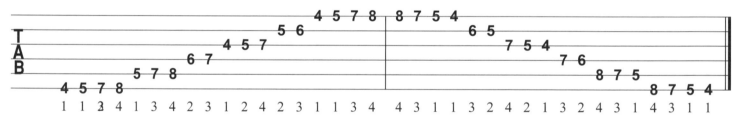

4th Position

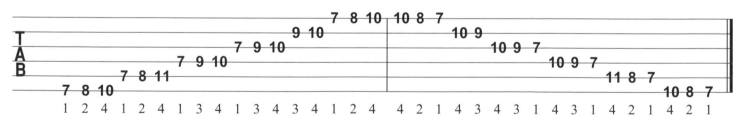

5th Position

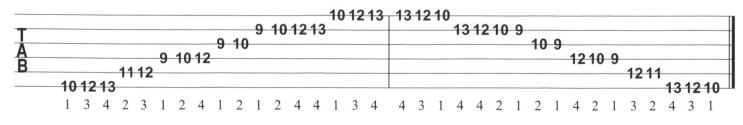

1st Position (octave)

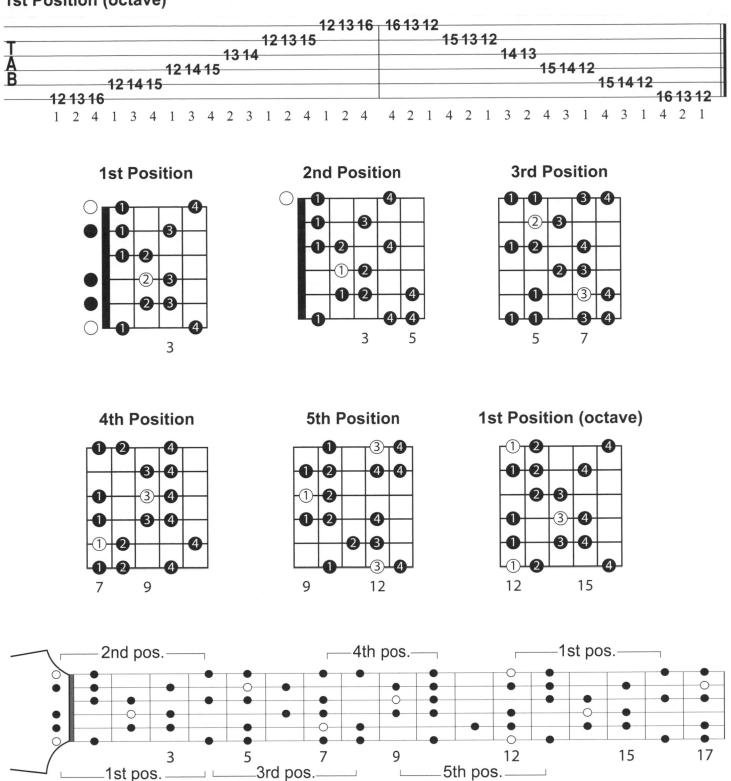

MUSIC ASSIGNMENT

Here is a simple rhythm focusing on the root note that you can use to apply these scales; it's a slow galloping rhythm using an open E power chord. A rhythm like this allows the guitar player freedom to play virtually any scale with the root E over it. Play the Phrygian major scales over this progression and get familiar with their sound and using them to create leads and melodies.

Bach Invention No. 13

This Bach invention is a great example of counterpoint melodies. This is a technique of combining two or more melodic lines in a way that they establish a harmonic relationship while still retaining their own individual melodic sense. Learn each line then play them together using the backing track.

Guitar 1

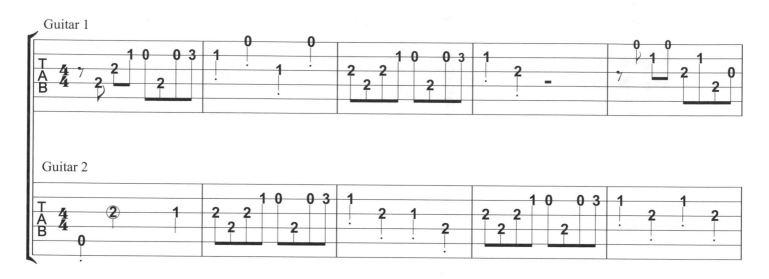

Guitar 2

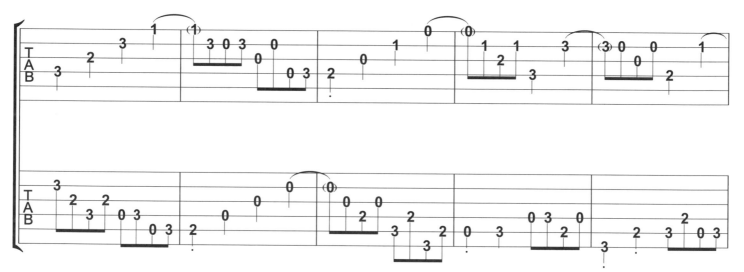

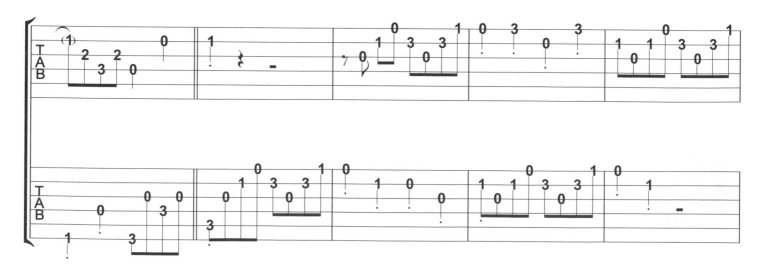

Bach Invention No.13
Page 2

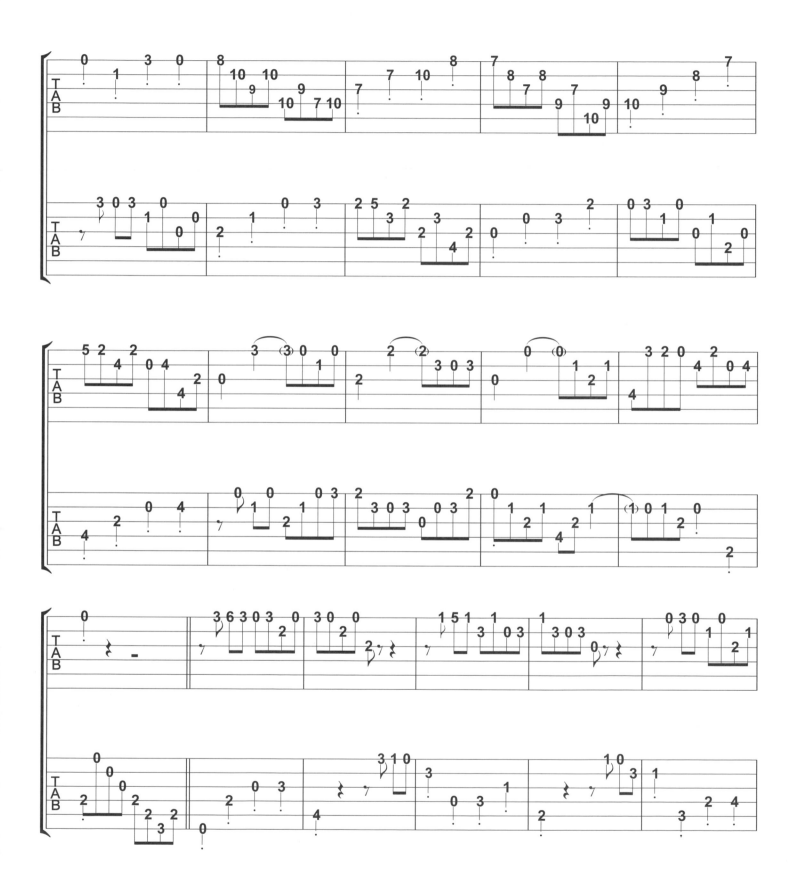

Bach Invention No.13
Page 3

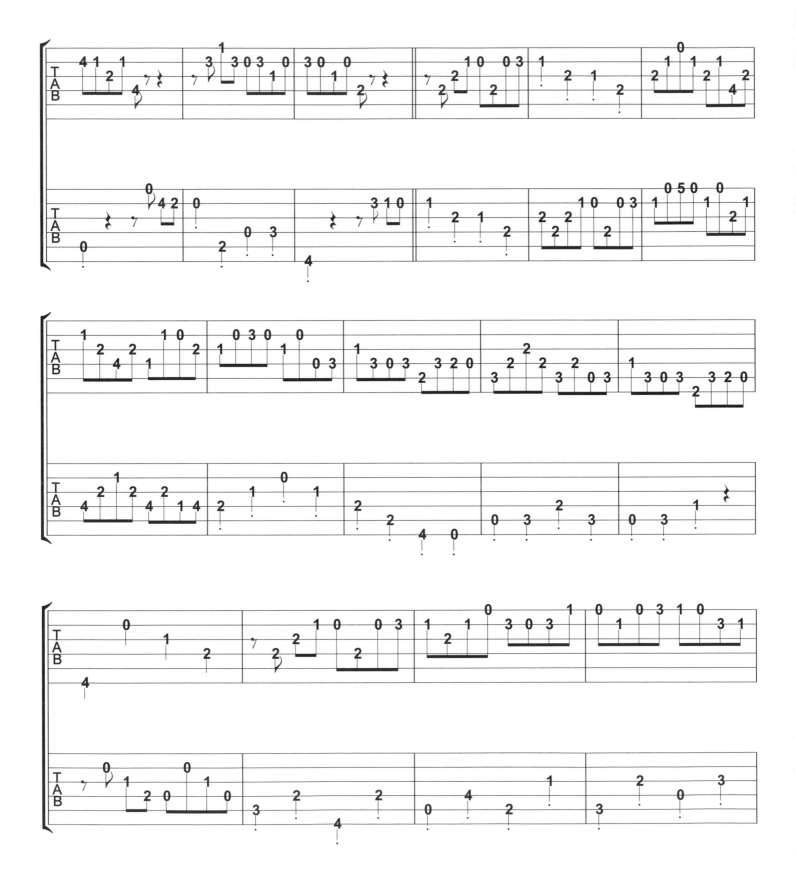

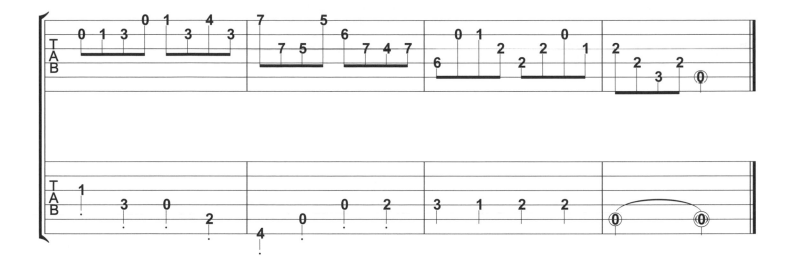

Arpeggio Progression - Crossing the Road

In this lesson you will learn how you can combine arpeggios to create a progression. As you play through the piece you can hear the chord changes outlined by each arpeggio. I recommend that you learn each arpeggio separately first then play them all in a row.

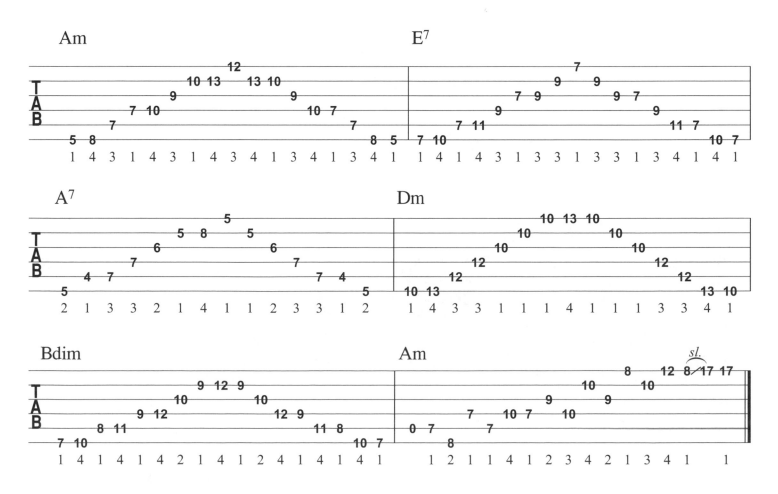

Learn Guitar 3 - Quiz 3

Congratulations you've made it to the end of Book 3! Go to RockHouseSchool.com and take the quiz to track your progress. You will receive an email with your results and an official Rock House Method "Certificate of Completion" when you pass.

Appendix

Full Major Scales

A Major

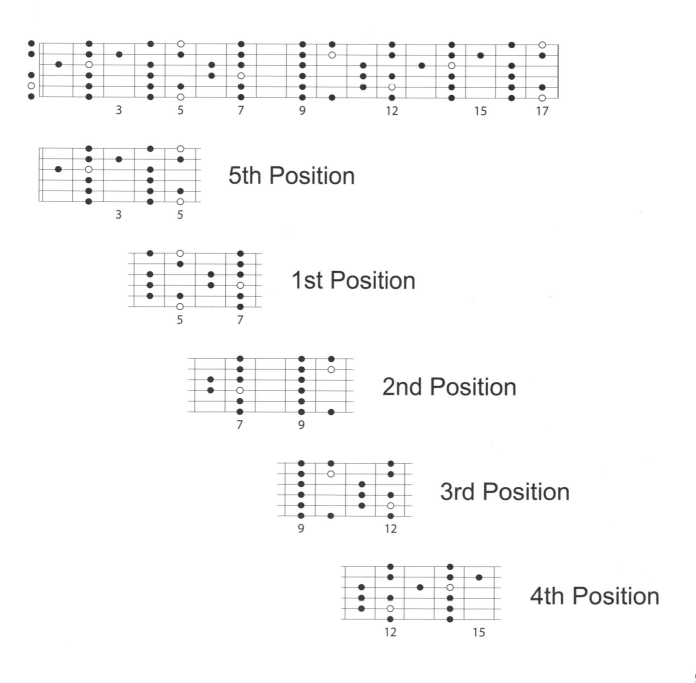

All Keys Relative Minor

C Major
C D E F G A B C D E F G A
A Minor

G Major
G A B C D E F# G A B C D E
E Minor

F Major
F G A B♭ C D E F G A B♭ C D
D Minor

D Major
D E F# G A B C# D E F# G A B
B Minor

B♭ Major
B♭ C D E♭ F G A B♭ C D E♭ F G
G Minor

A Major
A B C# D E F# G# A B C# D E F#
F# Minor

E♭ Major
E♭ F G A♭ B♭ C D E♭ F G A♭ B♭ C
C Minor

E Major
E F# G# A B C# D# E F# G# A B C#
C# Minor

A♭ Major
A♭ B♭ C D♭ E♭ F G A♭ B♭ C D♭ E♭ F
F Minor

B Major
B C# D# E F# G# A# B C# D# E F# G#
G# Minor

D♭ Major
D♭ E♭ F G♭ A♭ B♭ C D♭ E♭ F G♭ A♭ B♭
B♭ Minor

F# Major
F# G# A# B C# D# E# F# G# A# B C# D#
D# Minor

G♭ Major
G♭ A♭ B♭ C♭ D♭ E♭ F G♭ A♭ B♭ C♭ D♭ E♭
E♭ Minor

C# Major
C# D# E# F# G# A# B# C# D# E# F# G# A#
A# Minor

C♭ Major
C♭ D♭ E♭ F♭ G♭ A♭ B♭ C♭ D♭ E♭ F♭ G♭ A♭
A♭ Minor

Circle of 4th's and 5th's

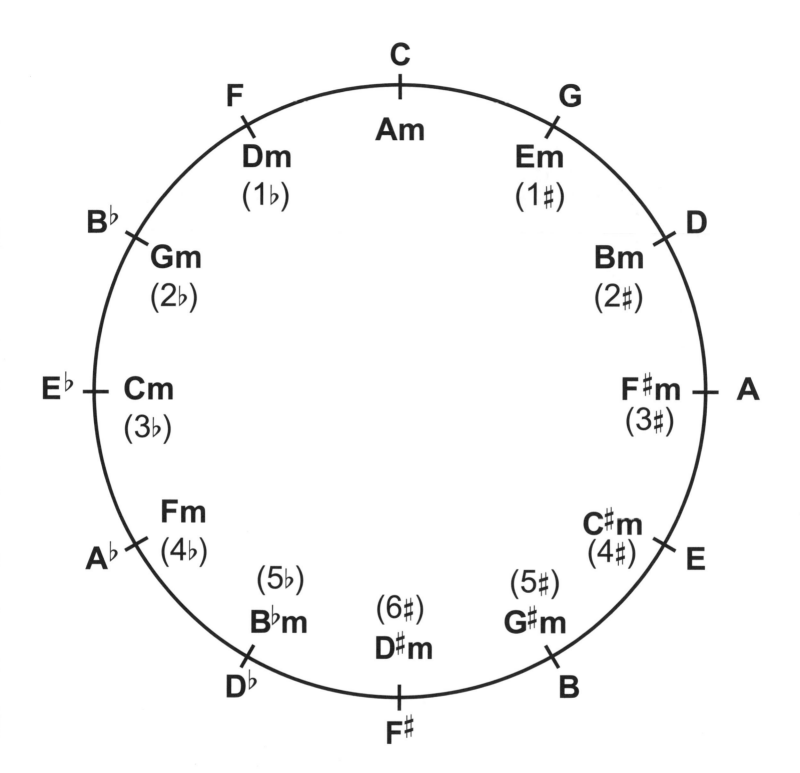

- Moving from C major to the left you move in fourths.
- Moving from C major to the right you move in fifths.
- Inside the circle is the relative minor scale for each adjacent key on the outside of the circle.

About the Author

John McCarthy
Creator of
The Rock House Method

John is the creator of The Rock House Method®, the world's leading musical instruction system. Over his 25 plus year career, he has written, produced and/or appeared in more than 100 instructional products. Millions of people around the world have learned to play music using John's easy-to-follow, accelerated programs.

John is a virtuoso musician who has worked with some of the industry's most legendary entertainers. He has the ability to break down, teach and communicate music in a manner that motivates and inspires others to achieve their dreams of playing an instrument.

As a musician and songwriter, John blends together a unique style of rock, metal, funk and blues in a collage of melodic compositions. Throughout his career, John has recorded and performed with renowned musicians including Doug Wimbish (Joe Satriani, Living Colour, The Rolling Stones, Madonna, Annie Lennox), Grammy Winner Leo Nocentelli, Rock & Roll Hall of Fame inductees Bernie Worrell and Jerome "Big Foot" Brailey, Freekbass, Gary Hoey, Bobby Kimball, David Ellefson (founding member of seven time Grammy nominee Megadeth), Will Calhoun (B.B. King, Mick Jagger and Paul Simon), Gus G of Ozzy and many more.

To get more information about John McCarthy, his music and his instructional products visit RockHouseSchool.com.